PRIORITIES, ROLES, AND GOALS

The Agenda 2018

MARC DICKERSON

AuthorHouse™
1663 Liberty Drive
Bloomington, IN 47403
www.authorhouse.com
Phone: 1 (800) 839-8640

© 2017 Marc Dickerson. All rights reserved.

No part of this book may be reproduced, stored in a retrieval system, or transmitted by any means without the written permission of the author.

Published by AuthorHouse   11/01/2017

ISBN: 978-1-5462-1473-1 (sc)
ISBN: 978-1-5462-1472-4 (e)

Library of Congress Control Number: 2017916519

Print information available on the last page.

Any people depicted in stock imagery provided by Thinkstock are models, and such images are being used for illustrative purposes only. Certain stock imagery © Thinkstock.

This book is printed on acid-free paper.

Because of the dynamic nature of the Internet, any web addresses or links contained in this book may have changed since publication and may no longer be valid. The views expressed in this work are solely those of the author and do not necessarily reflect the views of the publisher, and the publisher hereby disclaims any responsibility for them.

Priorities, Roles and Goals:

The Agenda

2018

Marc Dickerson

Priorities, Roles and Goals

I want to thank my parents, Ron and Penny, for all of the love and nurturing growing up and setting a strong foundation for my beliefs. Thank you to my wife, Mary Beth and two kids, Caden and Laine, for the motivation and support in making this book become possible. Thank you to all my family, coaches and teachers for instilling in me values, principles, morals and motivation. Without them, I would not be able to do this! Thank you Aunt Karen for your love, support and advice.

The Priorities, Roles and Goals Model

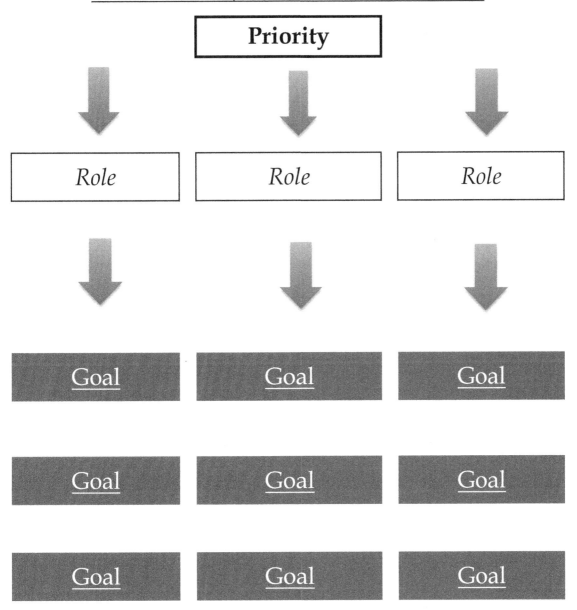

Success!!

Table of Contents

Personal Information	5		November	155
Introduction	6		December	167
Priorities	10		Useful Information	181
Roles	12		Future Planning	182
Goals	16		Medical Information	186
My Complete PRG Program	20		Personal Profile Sheet	187
PRG: The Agenda	*23*		Web Log	190
2017-2018 Calendar	24		Contacts	192
January	27		Journal	194
February	41		Goal Sheets	206
March	53			
April	65			
May	77			
June	91			
July	103			
August	117			
September	129			
October	141			

Thank you for purchasing PRG: <u>PRG: The Agenda</u>. What and how you schedule your day is very important. <u>The Agenda</u> will help you focus on what is important and if you are scheduling enough time in each priority, role and goal. Notice that the first day of each week starts with Monday and ends on Sunday.

*Feel free to contact me at **marc.dickerson@myprg.org** and visit my website at <u>www.myprg.org</u>.*

Personal Information

Name: _____

Address: _____
_____
_____
_____

Home Phone: _____
Cell Phone: _____

School / Work Information

School / Work _____

Address: _____
_____
_____
_____

Business Phone: _____
ID: _____

Birthday:	Anniversary:

Medial Alert Information

Medical Conditions _____
Food Allergies: _____
Drug Allergies: _____
Other: _____

In Case of Emergency Contact:

Name	Name	Name
Number	Number	Number

Emergency Contacts

Local Police

State Police

Fire Department

Ambulance

Hospital / ER

Poison Control

ATF

FBI

Suicide Prevention

Domestic Abuse

Other:

Other:

Other:

Other:

Chapter One

Introduction

It is easy to organize a desk, a notebook or even a garage. But how easy is it to organize your life? Where do you start? How do you know what is important to you? In this program, I will give you three steps to organizing your life. The **Priorities, Roles, and Goals** (PRG) program is the "Gateway" to helping you in many areas of your life. Establishing your **priorities** is the first step. Knowing your **roles** is the second step. Setting your **goals** is the third step. After completing the three steps, you will be able to identify areas of your life that you are not paying enough attention to. Certain priorities or roles may need to get dropped if you are overcrowding your life. People of all ages drift through life without direction and they do not realize the untapped potential that they may have. They do not have a sense of purpose or they lack direction about what is important to them. They do not realize that what they do now will affect their future. This plan is designed to help guide young teens and adults toward a more organized life.

My intent with PRG is for you to establish the direction you want your life to go and get you on a pathway to a productive life. Whether you are 15, 50, or any age; the priorities, roles and goals you select are based on your inner core principles and values.

Connect Your PRGs

Establish your priorities, know your roles, and set your goals. Your priorities, roles and goals all must mesh together based on the principles and values that you set for yourself. In this program, you will establish your priorities first. Think about the areas of your life that are most important to you. Once you have established your priorities, you will then take a look at what roles you play in each of your priorities. Ask yourself: What role do I take on in each of my priorities? Who am I? Once you have established your roles, you move to setting goals for each role that you play. This will make your roles and priorities successful. All three areas must interconnect and they each stem from one another.

Example:

Priority - School

Role - Student

Goal - Grades

Goal - Attendance

Goal - Graduate

Confidence-

A. A belief or conviction that an outcome will be favorable
B. Belief in the certainty of something
C. Belief in the effectiveness on one's own abilities or in one's favorable acceptance by others;
D. Trust or faith in a person or thing
E. A trusting relationship own abilities

http://ahdictionary.com

PRG will give you an overall outlook on your life; you will still need to posses other characteristics to be a successful person. **Passion** *is the key for success.* **Passion** *is the burning desire to do something within you. Setting up your program will give you the* **confidence** *to go forward and have a clear understanding of what is important to you. Having* **confidence** *in yourself and what you are doing is a key ingredient to being successful.*

Passion-

A. Strong or powerful emotion
B. A powerful emotion, such as anger or joy
C. Boundless enthusiasm
D. The object of such enthusiasm

Spiritual, Mental, and Physical Health

When setting up your PRG program, you must encompass your spiritual, mental and physical health. A weekly spiritual goal for someone of the Christian faith may be to memorize one Bible verse and attend church on a weekly basis. Mental goals are taking time for yourself to relax and clear your head. It could be meditating or reading a book or even going on a vacation. Physical goals could include working out, jogging or anything that will elevate your blood pressure to relieve everyday stress. When you first set up your program, integrate these three essential ingredients. Without having spiritual, mental and physical health, you will not be able to effectively fulfill your priorities, roles or goals. Make sure that you schedule time for each of these on your calendar.

> ## Establish your Priorities, Know your Roles, Set your Goals

Organizing your PRGs into Your Schedule

When you set up your daily, weekly or monthly schedule, it is essential that you make sure you schedule your time around your priorities, roles and goals. It is important that you see where your PRGs are scheduled. Check to see if you are giving enough time to your main priorities or if you are drifting off course. Setting your schedule and sticking to it is one way to monitor how you are doing with what is important to you.

Being Flexible

Being flexible means that you are able to drop what you are doing and focus your attention elsewhere. If an emergency situation comes up, be prepared to shift gears, even if it is not an item on your priority list. If a friend or a family member encounters a crisis situation, be ready to help and serve in that situation. As a teacher, when a tragic event happens that may affect your students, it would be a time to be flexible and to discuss that situation with your students. When crisis situations arise, you may have to adopt new roles, sometimes unfamiliar, as the situation demand. Crisis situations demand times of flexibility. You may have to temporarily stray from your PRG's.

Finding Your Niche

Answering these questions will help you find your niche in life. Constructing your PRG Program will help you identify your niche. In life, it is imperative that you take a look at yourself and ask what you are good at, what you like to do and where your best potential lay? Think about the talents that you posses. Do you know what they are? Sometimes it takes a long time to figure it out and it may require several re-evaluations of yourself. What you need to understand is that when you do figure out what you want to do with yourself; you have already set yourself up to be able to do that thing. Some students go through high school not sure as to what they want to be, so they do not take their education seriously. By the time they are seniors and decide that they want to go to college, they may have closed the doors on a lot of opportunities because they had not studied hard enough or had not received adequate grades throughout their high school career. Even if you do not know what you want to do, continue to work hard so that when you do figure it out, you will have a huge list of opportunities you may choose from. Do not limit your opportunities.

> *Create opportunities for yourself. The obstacles in your life are simply opportunities waiting to happen. Take on those obstacles full force and do not let them stand in your way.*

Reviewing Your PRG's

Reviewing your PRGs is going to be essential to maintaining your program. Some of your PRGs are going to change periodically. The priorities that you establish may not change unless you have an event in your life that dictates otherwise, such as a new job, graduating or other adventures that you need to devote more time to. Your roles will change on occasion but may still fit under your priorities. Roles will get adjusted from time to time and there will be constant re-evaluation around what is really important and what is really necessary. Goals will change based on short term and long term goals. Some goals are set for the rest of your life, but some short term goals could last for less than a week depending on what the goal is. Thus, you constantly think about how you may improve your PRG's.

Contacts

Going through life, hopefully, you will understand how essential it is to make contacts and to get to know people. You have often heard the saying "It's not what you know, but who you know." If this is true, getting to know people and establishing contacts will help you. The reverse is also true, as people may reach out to you for help and you could be a valuable contact for them! Create a resource file with names, how you know them, and how to contact them. A resource file or address book may be used as a reference when you run into trouble or need to contact a friend or an associate.

Let's Get Started

In the blank area below write down   1. **What is important to you?**   2. **Who are you?**   3. **What do you want in life?**

This will be the beginning of **YOUR** Program

Chapter Two

Priorities

```
                    Definition
n. pl. pri·or·i·ties
1  Precedence, especially established by order of
   importance or urgency.
2  a. An established right to precedence.
   b. An authoritative rating that establishes such precedenc
3  A preceding or coming earlier in time.
4  Something afforded or deserving prior attention.
                http://ahdictionary.com/
```

The first step to your program is to establish your priorities. When you establish your priorities, you figure out what is most important and meaningful to you. These are the people and activities that you consider the most important in your life. When you decide what your top seven priorities are, you may spend at least 95% of your waking day in those priorities. Priorities set the tone for the rest of this program. On certain days, more time may be devoted to one priority than to another. Flexibility enters here, some priorities may receive different amounts of daily attention.

Again, your priorities encompass your spiritual, mental, and physical health. Keep in consideration your general well-being.

Types of Priorities

Priorities are areas of topics in your life that are important to you: e.g. Spirituality, Family, Work, Friends, Finances, Education, Health, Leisure, Shopping, Cooking, Cleaning, Yourself, Coaching, Athletics, etc.

Establishing Your Priorities

Think about the areas of your life where you spend a lot of time or areas where you *should or would like* to focus your time. Three things should influence your priorities: 1. how important it is to you, 2. how much time are you willing to spend and 3. how much money are you willing to invest.

```
Priorities:

Importance

Time

Money
```

```
Go ahead and think about your priorities and list them.  List several.
_____     _____     _____
_____     _____     _____
_____     _____     _____
_____     _____     _____
```

* Your first priority will be the most important, an overriding force in your life. This must be very important to you. What do you center your life around? Or how do you spend your time?

 * Your most important priorities will be at the top of the list.

* Some priorities may merge together or become roles. We will see this as we establish some of our priorities and develop your program. This process will take time and different scenarios until you are comfortable with your program.

Rank Your Top Seven Priorities

1 _____

2 _____

3 _____

4 _____

5 _____

6 _____

7 _____

Some Things to Think About…..

Set priorities and stick to them as often as possible, but be flexible because different events in your life will change your priorities. For example, these situations will change your priorities: marriage, death, crisis situation, etc. Also realize that some priorities are permanent and some are temporary. School should definitely be a top priority, but after you graduate and become part of the work force, it may drop low on your list unless you decide to further your education.

From Priorities to Roles

In the next section we will move from priorities to roles. In each of your priorities, you will list several roles that will fulfill your priorities.

Chapter Three

Roles

Definition
n. rōl
1   The characteristic and expected social behavior of an individual.
http://ahdictionary.com/

    The second part of your program is to know your personal roles. The roles you take on are derived from your priorities. This section will focus on the different roles and responsibilities that you take on. A role or a responsibility is the expected social behavior and position that you take. For example, what is expected of you if you are a parent, coach, organization leader, or a student? What do people see when they look at you? What is the expected social behavior? Do you agree with it? The role you take and how you act in your role may affect other people. You must take care and understand your role and what is expected of you in that role. How can you be successful in that particular role? Well, by observing and learning. I believe you can learn from anybody or anything on this planet. Take a look at positive and successful people. Think about what makes them positive and successful. What types of Positive Principles, Quality Characteristics, and Ethical Values do they posses? I also believe you can look at the opposite and learn from that as well. You may take the worst person in the world and learn from that person. What you may learn is what not to do or how that person has negatively affected other people's lives. Focus on behaviors that you desire. Keep in mind that your behavior does affect other people. Your roles may change with different events in your life. For example, you may get a new job, promotion, new child, etc.

    If one of your priorities is family, you may have several roles to fulfill to make that priority successful. The roles that you may have are father, mother, husband, wife, son, daughter, brother, sister, and other such roles used for maintaining a stable living environment, such as doing house chores, managing money, etc.

    One of our main roles in life is to serve others and that may be why we were placed on this earth. If you have the concept of "what can I do for others?" then you may be on your way to a pleasing life. There are several ways in which we may be useful to others, whether it be financially, time, physical labor, or even counseling, among other ways of being a help.

    Fulfilling roles may take a lot of leadership on your part and it may involve teamwork with others. You may not be able to be successful by yourself. Be willing to reach out to others and make sure that others are able to reach out to you, as well.

    Be aware of positive and negative roles. Do not get caught up in negative roles such as a person who is not willing to help, who gossips, etc. Usually, you do not assign yourself to these roles, but others may. They count also.

> *The most import asset you have is TIME. Giving YOUR time to other people leaves a life-lasting impact.*

Defining Your Roles

What are the roles you that play in your life? When people look at you, what do they see? Mother, Father, Son, Daughter, Coach, Teacher, Boss, President, Doctor, Nurse, Mechanic, Student, Player, Leader, etc. In your family are you looked upon to do finances, chores, etc. These are responsibilities that are found in some priorities.

Think about everything that you do in a week or a months' time. List all of the different roles that you play. Do not leave out any role, as small as it may be, or even if it is an infrequent role. List all of the roles that pertain to you. Keep in mind the different roles that you have associated with from your priority list. Very important – ask yourself "How do these roles fit in with my priorities?"

Go ahead and think about your roles and list them. List several.

_____   _____   _____

_____   _____   _____

_____   _____   _____

_____   _____   _____

Positive Principles, Quality Characteristics, and Ethical Values

Positive Principles are what you believe; they are the guiding force for which you base your decisions. You base your **Positive Principles** on a moral compass. If you base your principles on other people, they may let you down. If you base your principles on money, it may let you down. If you base your principles on any material object, it may let you down. The same is true for any material possessions that you think is important.   If you need a nice car, a nice house, and other material objects to feel good about yourself, you are setting yourself up for failure and will neglect other important parts of your life. What would happen if one day you lost everything that you have? Would you be unable to move on? That is why you base your principles on non-material concepts that cannot be taken away from you.

Honesty is an important principle to have. Are you confident enough to have courage of your convictions? Are you able to tell the truth no matter what the consequences are? Being *loyal* is another positive principle. Being a loyal person means that you will go to war or stand up for certain people or groups. You will do whatever you may need to do in order to support their needs. Being *respectful* and *courteous* are other positive principles to posses. Having the *courage* to stand up for what you believe will also shape who you are. Are you willing to lay it on the line for your beliefs? These words are easy to say, but how do you really implement these principles in your life?

Definition
Principle -
A. A rule or standard, especially of good behavior
B. The collectivity of moral or ethical standards or judgments
Character -
A. The combination of mental characteristics and behavior that distinguishing a person or group
B. The distinguishing nature of something
C   Moral strength; integrity
D   Public estimation of someone; reputation
Values-
A. Of great importance, use, or service
B. Having admirable or esteemed qualities
http://ahdictionary.com/

Quality Characteristics is who you are. To be successful in these roles, we need to have certain types of **Quality Characteristics** that are positive and productive in order to fulfill these roles. You can actually see these characteristics displayed in people. Think of the influential people in your life. Maybe you know someone who you may have grown up with that you felt was a very caring or helpful person and that person made you feel special. Maybe you had a coach that was a great leader and teacher. These are the types of quality characteristics that you may strive to have. Some examples of the roles of those people that are successful may be that they are leaders, listeners, humble, able to solve problems, etc. If you want to be a good student or co-worker, you will need to have several Quality Characteristics such as being a good listener, researcher, studious, and willing to behave in a certain way. Take a look at other students or people who are successful. What do they have that helps them to be successful?

Ethical Values are what is important to you. What do you value in life? Your set of **Ethical Values** will positively affect your roles and relationships with others. If you value getting to work on time, it will have a positive effect with your relationship with your boss. On the other hand, if you are late and do not value being on time, your job could be in jeopardy. If you are a trustworthy friend, you will be able to maximize friendships and relationships.

Think about people that have Positive Principles, Quality Characteristics, and Ethical Values that you respect and those traits that you admire in them. Be observant for some of the characteristics you may need to be successful.

Think about people that have Positive Principles, Quality Characteristics and Ethical Values that you admire.	
Name	*Principle, Characteristic or Value that you admire*

Putting it Together

Take each role you have defined for yourself from page 23 and see if you are able to place them in your top seven priorities. You may realize some other roles that you play after looking at your priorities. For example, if you listed your family as a priority, a role that you could have is that of a son, father, mother, aunt, etc. With each role, think about Positive Principles, Quality Characteristics, and Ethical Values you need to nurture each of those roles.

> *Example:*
> **Priority** - Family
> *Role* - Son
>
> Principles,
> Characteristics, Values
> 1. Good Listener
> 2. Respectful
> 3. Thoughtful
> 4. Honesty

For each role you chose, you will have strengths and weakness in that role. It is important to know and understand what you are good at and what you need to work on skills to be successful in that role. When understanding your roles, take a good look at your self and identify areas of strengths and weaknesses when you set up your program.

In the roles you take, remember to be yourself, look at the positive characteristics of others, and always **be true to yourself**. You should end up with about 20 to 30 roles at the most, as more could be considered overloading.

In the next section we are going to move from roles to setting goals for each of the roles that you have.

Chapter Four

Goals

Definition
n. (gōl)
1 The object toward which an endeavor is directed; an end.
http://ahdictionary.com/

Setting Goals

Setting your goals is the third and final part of this program. Setting goals is a basic fundamental part of life. This is where your program comes alive! You realistically should set goals that match your priorities and roles. Goals will establish direction in your life. To set goals, look at your roles and ask yourself, "What goals do I need to set to be successful in this role, and how will my priority and role benefit from this goal?" Some goals may be long-term, short-term, or daily goals. The "goal setting" area is where you will want to really focus and encompass your spiritual, mental, and physical health.

> *The "goal setting" area is where you will want to really focus and encompass your spiritual, mental, and physical health.*

Definition
Desire -
A. The feeling of wanting to have something or wishing that something will happen.
B. An instance of this feeling.
Dedication –
A. The act of dedicating or the state of being dedicated.
B. Selfless devotion
Determination –
A. Firmness of purpose; resolve
B. A fixed intention or resolution.
http://ahdictionary.com/

Like your priorities, when setting goals, take into consideration the amount of time, money and energy you are willing to use on that goal. You will then have to determine if it is worthwhile or not. Once you set your goals, become committed to obtaining that goal. Personally, I like to use the three D's after I have set a goal: **Desire, Dedication, and Determination.**

Don't let obstacles or people tell you that you may not reach your goal. Go after that goal using the three D's. Another thing to think about is that you do not want to set new goals and begin to lose focus over the older goals that you had already had set. Keep in mind your priorities and roles that help set up the goals.

Make use of your calendar in your agenda section in order to keep your focus and to be well rounded with your PRG's.

If one of your roles is "health", which could fall under your "Me" priority, the goals you set for being healthy could be to lose weight, work out a certain number of times in a week, get a physical once per year or have your blood pressure at a desirable level just to name a few.

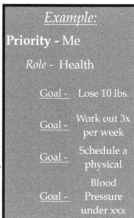

Example:

Priority - Me

Role - Health

Goal - Lose 10 lbs.

Goal - Work out 3x per week

Goal - Schedule a physical

Goal - Blood Pressure under xxx

Use Goals to Solve Problems

We encounter problems just about every day of our lives. Some problems are major and some are minor. The great thing about goal setting is that you may take those problems and begin to set goals in order to overcome them or to fix them.

For some problems, you may need to come up with several different "game plans" if the first few solutions do not work. You may have to adjust your goals to continue to work on the problems. **Problems are opportunities in disguise**. Use goals to solve problems. For example, let's say that you are not passing a class. How can you set short-range goals that will affect the outcome of your grade? You could set daily goals for extra study, get extra help from a teacher, and do practice problems every day. These daily or short range goals will have an effect on your final long range goal, which is for your final grade to be passable.

> 1. You get yourself motivated to have the *desire* to obtain the goal.
>
> 2. You get yourself motivated to be *dedicated* to the goal.
>
> 3. You get yourself motivated to be *determined* to reach that goal.

It is very possible to end up with about 90 or so goals that you will be working on at one time. This is why planning and organizing is a very important part of your life. If you feel that you have too many goals then narrow them down. Do not let too many goals create a situation that would not allow you to be successful in any of the goals.

Types of Goals

A. Daily Goals

1 Goals you set each day to accomplish.

2 May be smaller steps toward short and long term goals. Refer to your steps and time-line of events on your short and long term goal sheets.

3 May be just daily things that you might want to get done.

4 Align with daily Spiritual, Mental, and Physical goals. This is where your calendar really comes into use. You may quickly want to see if you are setting enough spiritual, mental, and physical goals each day or each week.

   a. Daily Spiritual goal may be to go to church, read a verse from the bible, pray, discuss your spirituality with someone.

   b. Daily Mental goal may be to meditate, relax, read a book, or talk with a friend.

   c. Daily Physical goals may be to run, walk, ride a bike, lift weights, work in the yard, or even complete a research paper.

B. Short-Term Goals

1 Goals that you may want to obtain weekly or within the next few months.

2 Short-term goals may be pieces of your long term goals. Refer to your steps and time line of events.

C. Long-Term Goals

1 Goals that you want to obtain in the future: 6 months, 1 year, 3 years, 5 years or longer down the road.

2 Long-term goals could be lifelong goals

Behaviors, Attitudes and Situations

When you set a goal, make sure you fully understand what will help you to reach your goal, but it is just as important to understand behaviors, attitudes and different situations that will positively or negatively affect your goal. Make a list, like a "pros / cons" list of **Behaviors, Attitudes, and Situations (BAS)** that will impact your goals in a positive and/or negative way.

For example, if you have a goal of being an All-State athlete, your list may look like this....

Positive BAS (Behaviors, Attitudes, Situations)

1. Lift weights

2. Study and get good grades

3. Be coachable

4. Attend school

5. Attend practice and be on time

6. Have a positive attitude

7. Respect my coaches and teammates

8. Do not hang out with people who may get me in trouble

Negative BAS (Behaviors, Attitudes, Situations)

1. Do not give 100% in the classroom and at practice

2. Do not study and do classwork

3. Have a negative attitude

4. Show disrespect to teachers and coaches

5. Hang out with others who DO NOT share my same goals and beliefs

Components of Goal Setting

1. Identify what Priority and Role your goal is aligned with. Set a start date and a completion date. Identify if this is a daily goal, short-term goal, or a long-term goal. Set your goal! Ask yourself, "Why is it important to set this goal?"

2. Make a list of what you need to do in order to obtain this goal and what needs to get done to make this goal successful.

3. Steps/Time line of events - What steps do you need to take to achieve your goal? Set a time line of events to give you direction and purpose. You may want to draft a list on the notes section and go back a make changes where needed.

4. People who may help – Seek out people who may help you achieve your goal. Use your resource file of people. You may not be able to do it alone.

5. Follow up – Follow up your goal with notes, what you could change about the process, what worked and did not work, etc.

6. Next Steps - What needs to be done next in order to advance this goal or for this goal to be tied into another goal?

Goal Tips

1. Be specific with your goals and make sure they have a purpose and are reasonable and attainable.

2. Be consistent with your goals in terms that they are realistic.

3. With your goals, what are you sacrificing to obtain this goal? Is it worth it? Check your priorities.

4. Make goals that are measurable and concrete. Look back at your goal and actually see it or collect data to show improvement.

5. Turn your problems into goals. If you are having problems and troubles, create goals to fix them. They may be long or short and integrate daily goals to help the problems.

6. What are the problem areas of your life? How may they be corrected? Come up with a plan – use a goal sheet.

7. Your goals need to have a timeline of smaller goals working toward your main goal.

The bottom line is.....let positive people help you to obtain your goals!

My Complete PRG Program

Priority #1	Priority #2	Priority #3	Priority #4

Priority #1

Role #1:

	Goals
1	
2	
3	

Role #2:

	Goals
1	
2	
3	

Role #3:

	Goals
1	
2	
3	

Role #4:

	Goals
1	
2	
3	

Role #5:

	Goals
1	
2	
3	

Role #6:

	Goals
1	
2	
3	

Priority #2

Role #1:

	Goals
1	
2	
3	

Role #2:

	Goals
1	
2	
3	

Role #3:

	Goals
1	
2	
3	

Role #4:

	Goals
1	
2	
3	

Role #5:

	Goals
1	
2	
3	

Role #6:

	Goals
1	
2	
3	

Priority #3

Role #1:

	Goals
1	
2	
3	

Role #2:

	Goals
1	
2	
3	

Role #3:

	Goals
1	
2	
3	

Role #4:

	Goals
1	
2	
3	

Role #5:

	Goals
1	
2	
3	

Role #6:

	Goals
1	
2	
3	

Priority #4

Role #1:

	Goals
1	
2	
3	

Role #2:

	Goals
1	
2	
3	

Role #3:

	Goals
1	
2	
3	

Role #4:

	Goals
1	
2	
3	

Role #5:

	Goals
1	
2	
3	

Role #6:

	Goals
1	
2	
3	

Priority #5	Priority #6	Priority #7

Role #1:

Goals		Goals		Goals	
1		1		1	
2		2		2	
3		3		3	

Role #2:

Goals		Goals		Goals	
1		1		1	
2		2		2	
3		3		3	

Role #3:

Goals		Goals		Goals	
1		1		1	
2		2		2	
3		3		3	

Role #4:

Goals		Goals		Goals	
1		1		1	
2		2		2	
3		3		3	

Role #5:

Goals		Goals		Goals	
1		1		1	
2		2		2	
3		3		3	

Role #6:

Goals		Goals		Goals	
1		1		1	
2		2		2	
3		3		3	

You can't wait for inspiration. You have to go after it with a club.

Jack London

Priorities,

Roles,

and <u>Goals</u>:

<u>The Agenda</u>

2018

2018

JANUARY
M	T	W	T	F	S	S
1	2	3	4	5	6	7
8	9	10	11	12	13	14
15	16	17	18	19	20	21
22	23	24	25	26	27	28
29	30	31				

FEBRUARY
M	T	W	T	F	S	S
			1	2	3	4
5	6	7	8	9	10	11
12	13	14	15	16	17	18
19	20	21	22	23	24	25
26	27	28				

MARCH
M	T	W	T	F	S	S
			1	2	3	4
5	6	7	8	9	10	11
12	13	14	15	16	17	18
19	20	21	22	23	24	25
26	27	28	29	30	31	

APRIL
M	T	W	T	F	S	S
						1
2	3	4	5	6	7	8
9	10	11	12	13	14	15
16	17	18	19	20	21	22
23	24	25	26	27	28	29
30						

MAY
M	T	W	T	F	S	S
	1	2	3	4	5	6
7	8	9	10	11	12	13
14	15	16	17	18	19	20
21	22	23	24	25	26	27
28	29	30	31			

JUNE
M	T	W	T	F	S	S
				1	2	3
4	5	6	7	8	9	10
11	12	13	14	15	16	17
18	19	20	21	22	23	24
25	26	27	28	29	30	

JULY
M	T	W	T	F	S	S
						1
2	3	4	5	6	7	8
9	10	11	12	13	14	15
16	17	18	19	20	21	22
23	24	25	26	27	28	29
30	31					

AUGUST
M	T	W	T	F	S	S
		1	2	3	4	5
6	7	8	9	10	11	12
13	14	15	16	17	18	19
20	21	22	23	24	25	26
27	28	29	30	31		

SEPTEMBER
M	T	W	T	F	S	S
					1	2
3	4	5	6	7	8	9
10	11	12	13	14	15	16
17	18	19	20	21	22	23
24	25	26	27	28	29	30

OCTOBER
M	T	W	T	F	S	S
1	2	3	4	5	6	7
8	9	10	11	12	13	14
15	16	17	18	19	20	21
22	23	24	25	26	27	28
29	30	31				

NOVEMBER
M	T	W	T	F	S	S
			1	2	3	4
5	6	7	8	9	10	11
12	13	14	15	16	17	18
19	20	21	22	23	24	25
26	27	28	29	30		

DECEMBER
M	T	W	T	F	S	S
					1	2
3	4	5	6	7	8	9
10	11	12	13	14	15	16
17	18	19	20	21	22	23
24	25	26	27	28	29	30
31						

2019

JANUARY
M	T	W	T	F	S	S
	1	2	3	4	5	6
7	8	9	10	11	12	13
14	15	16	17	18	19	20
21	22	23	24	25	26	27
28	29	30	31			

FEBRUARY
M	T	W	T	F	S	S
				1	2	3
4	5	6	7	8	9	10
11	12	13	14	15	16	17
18	19	20	21	22	23	24
25	26	27	28			

MARCH
M	T	W	T	F	S	S
				1	2	3
4	5	6	7	8	9	10
11	12	13	14	15	16	17
18	19	20	21	22	23	24
25	26	27	28	29	30	31

APRIL
M	T	W	T	F	S	S
1	2	3	4	5	6	7
8	9	10	11	12	13	14
15	16	17	18	19	20	21
22	23	24	25	26	27	28
29	30					

MAY
M	T	W	T	F	S	S
		1	2	3	4	5
6	7	8	9	10	11	12
13	14	15	16	17	18	19
20	21	22	23	24	25	26
27	28	29	30	31		

JUNE
M	T	W	T	F	S	S
					1	2
3	4	5	6	7	8	9
10	11	12	13	14	15	16
17	18	19	20	21	22	23
24	25	26	27	28	29	30

JULY
M	T	W	T	F	S	S
1	2	3	4	5	6	7
8	9	10	11	12	13	14
15	16	17	18	19	20	21
22	23	24	25	26	27	28
29	30	31				

AUGUST
M	T	W	T	F	S	S
			1	2	3	4
5	6	7	8	9	10	11
12	13	14	15	16	17	18
19	20	21	22	23	24	25
26	27	28	29	30	31	

SEPTEMBER
M	T	W	T	F	S	S
						1
2	3	4	5	6	7	8
9	10	11	12	13	14	15
16	17	18	19	20	21	22
23	24	25	26	27	28	29
30						

OCTOBER
M	T	W	T	F	S	S
	1	2	3	4	5	6
7	8	9	10	11	12	13
14	15	16	17	18	19	20
21	22	23	24	25	26	27
28	29	30	31			

NOVEMBER
M	T	W	T	F	S	S
				1	2	3
4	5	6	7	8	9	10
11	12	13	14	15	16	17
18	19	20	21	22	23	24
25	26	27	28	29	30	

December
M	T	W	T	F	S	S
						1
2	3	4	5	6	7	8
9	10	11	12	13	14	15
16	17	18	19	20	21	22
23	24	25	26	27	28	29
30	31					

** Please note that in <u>The Agenda</u>, Monday is the first day of the week, Saturday and Sunday are the last days of the week.

> *Life is about making an impact, not making an income.*

–Kevin Kruse

Ability is what you're capable of doing. Motivation determines what you do. Attitude determines how well you do it.

Lou Holtz

January

Birthdays / Anniversaries / Other Important Dates

Date	Event	Date	Event
_____	_____	_____	_____
_____	_____	_____	_____
_____	_____	_____	_____
_____	_____	_____	_____

Priority Focuses For the Month:

_____

_____

_____

_____

_____

Role Focuses For the Month:

_____

_____

_____

_____

_____

Goal Focuses For the Month:

_____

_____

_____

_____

_____

People I Need to Contact This Month

_____   _____

_____   _____

_____   _____

January 2018

Monday	Tuesday	Wednesday	Thursday
1	2	3	4
8	9	10	11
15	16	17	18
22	23	24	25
29	30	31	Notes:

PRG PRG PRG PRG

Friday	Saturday	Sunday	Notes / Focus
5	6	7	
12	13	14	
19	20	21	
26	27	28	

Notes:

January 1 - 7

2018

Monday
1

Tuesday
2

Wednesday
3

Thursday
4

Priority #1	Priority #2	Priority #3	Priority #4

December
M	T	W	T	F	S	S
				1	2	3
4	5	6	7	8	9	10
11	12	13	14	15	16	17
18	19	20	21	22	23	24
25	26	27	28	29	30	31

JANUARY
M	T	W	T	F	S	S
1	2	3	4	5	6	7
8	9	10	11	12	13	14
15	16	17	18	19	20	21
22	23	24	25	26	27	28
29	30	31				

FEBRUARY
M	T	W	T	F	S	S
				1	2	3	4
5	6	7	8	9	10	11
12	13	14	15	16	17	18
19	20	21	22	23	24	25
26	27	28				

Friday
5

Saturday
6

Sunday
7

Notes:

Priority #5	Priority #6	Priority #7	Goal Focus:

Monday

8

Tuesday

9

Wednesday

10

Thursday

11

Priority #1	Priority #2	Priority #3	Priority #4

December						
M	T	W	T	F	S	S
				1	2	3
4	5	6	7	8	9	10
11	12	13	14	15	16	17
18	19	20	21	22	23	24
25	26	27	28	29	30	31

JANUARY						
M	T	W	T	F	S	S
1	2	3	4	5	6	7
8	9	10	11	12	13	14
15	16	17	18	19	20	21
22	23	24	25	26	27	28
29	30	31				

FEBRUARY						
M	T	W	T	F	S	S
			1	2	3	4
5	6	7	8	9	10	11
12	13	14	15	16	17	18
19	20	21	22	23	24	25
26	27	28				

Friday
12

Saturday
13

Sunday
14

Notes:

Priority #5	Priority #6	Priority #7	Goal Focus:

Monday	
15	

Tuesday	
16	

Wednesday	
17	

Thursday	
18	

Priority #1	Priority #2	Priority #3	Priority #4

December								JANUARY								FEBRUARY					
M	T	W	T	F	S	S		M	T	W	T	F	S	S		M	T	W	T	F	S	S
				1	2	3		1	2	3	4	5	6	7						1	2	3	4
4	5	6	7	8	9	10		8	9	10	11	12	13	14		5	6	7	8	9	10	11
11	12	13	14	15	16	17		15	16	17	18	19	20	21		12	13	14	15	16	17	18
18	19	20	21	22	23	24		22	23	24	25	26	27	28		19	20	21	22	23	24	25
25	26	27	28	29	30	31		29	30	31						26	27	28				

Friday
19

Saturday
20

Sunday
21

Notes:

Priority #5	Priority #6	Priority #7	Goal Focus:

Monday

22

Tuesday

23

Wednesday

24

Thursday

25

Priority #1	Priority #2	Priority #3	Priority #4

December							
M	T	W	T	F	S	S
				1	2	3
4	5	6	7	8	9	10
11	12	13	14	15	16	17
18	19	20	21	22	23	24
25	26	27	28	29	30	31

JANUARY							
M	T	W	T	F	S	S
1	2	3	4	5	6	7
8	9	10	11	12	13	14
15	16	17	18	19	20	21
22	23	24	25	26	27	28
29	30	31				

FEBRUARY							
M	T	W	T	F	S	S
			1	2	3	4
5	6	7	8	9	10	11
12	13	14	15	16	17	18
19	20	21	22	23	24	25
26	27	28				

Friday
26

Saturday
27

Sunday
28

Notes:

Priority #5	Priority #6	Priority #7	Goal Focus:

Monday

29

Tuesday

30

Wednesday

31

Thursday

1

Priority #1	Priority #2	Priority #3	Priority #4

December						
M	T	W	T	F	S	S
				1	2	3
4	5	6	7	8	9	10
11	12	13	14	15	16	17
18	19	20	21	22	23	24
25	26	27	28	29	30	31

JANUARY						
M	T	W	T	F	S	S
1	2	3	4	5	6	7
8	9	10	11	12	13	14
15	16	17	18	19	20	21
22	23	24	25	26	27	28
29	30	31				

FEBRUARY						
M	T	W	T	F	S	S
				1	2	3	4
5	6	7	8	9	10	11
12	13	14	15	16	17	18
19	20	21	22	23	24	25
26	27	28				

Friday
2

Saturday
3

Sunday
4

Notes:

Priority #5	Priority #6	Priority #7	Goal Focus:

Notes / Monthly Review

_____
_____
_____
_____
_____
_____
_____
_____
_____
_____
_____
_____
_____
_____
_____
_____
_____
_____
_____
_____
_____
_____
_____
_____
_____
_____
_____
_____
_____
_____

February

Birthdays / Anniversaries / Other Important Dates

Date	Event	Date	Event
_____	_____	_____	_____
_____	_____	_____	_____
_____	_____	_____	_____
_____	_____	_____	_____

Priority Focuses For the Month:

_____

_____

_____

_____

_____

Role Focuses For the Month:

_____

_____

_____

_____

_____

Goal Focuses For the Month:

_____

_____

_____

_____

_____

People I Need to Contact This Month

_____ _____

_____ _____

_____ _____

February   2018

Monday	Tuesday	Wednesday	Thursday
Notes:			1
5	6	7	8
12	13	14	15
19	20	21	22
26	27	28	Notes:

The love of family and the admiration of friends is much more important than wealth and privilege. Charles Kuralt

Friday	Saturday	Sunday	Notes/Focus
2	3	4	
9	10	11	
16	17	18	
23	24	25	
Notes:			

Monday

5

Tuesday

6

Wednesday

7

Thursday

8

Priority #1	Priority #2	Priority #3	Priority #4

JANUARY	FEBRUARY	MARCH
M T W T F S S	M T W T F S S	M T W T F S S
1 2 3 4 5 6 7	1 2 3 4	1 2 3 4
8 9 10 11 12 13 14	5 6 7 8 9 10 11	5 6 7 8 9 10 11
15 16 17 18 19 20 21	12 13 14 15 16 17 18	12 13 14 15 16 17 18
22 23 24 25 26 27 28	19 20 21 22 23 24 25	19 20 21 22 23 24 25
29 30 31	26 27 28	26 27 28 29 30 31

Friday
9

Saturday
10

Sunday
11

Notes:

Priority #5	Priority #6	Priority #7	Goal Focus:

Monday

12

Tuesday

13

Wednesday

14

Thursday

15

Priority #1	Priority #2	Priority #3	Priority #4

	JANUARY								FEBRUARY								MARCH					
M	T	W	T	F	S	S		M	T	W	T	F	S	S		M	T	W	T	F	S	S
1	2	3	4	5	6	7					1	2	3	4					1	2	3	4
8	9	10	11	12	13	14		5	6	7	8	9	10	11		5	6	7	8	9	10	11
15	16	17	18	19	20	21		12	13	14	15	16	17	18		12	13	14	15	16	17	18
22	23	24	25	26	27	28		19	20	21	22	23	24	25		19	20	21	22	23	24	25
29	30	31						26	27	28						26	27	28	29	30	31	

Friday
16

Saturday
17

Sunday
18

Notes:

Priority #5	Priority #6	Priority #7	Goal Focus:

February 19 - 25   *2018*

Monday
19

Tuesday
20

Wednesday
21

Thursday
22

Priority #1	**Priority #2**	**Priority #3**	**Priority #4**

JANUARY	FEBRUARY	MARCH
M T W T F S S	M T W T F S S	M T W T F S S
1 2 3 4 5 6 7	1 2 3 4	1 2 3 4
8 9 10 11 12 13 14	5 6 7 8 9 10 11	5 6 7 8 9 10 11
15 16 17 18 19 20 21	12 13 14 15 16 17 18	12 13 14 15 16 17 18
22 23 24 25 26 27 28	19 20 21 22 23 24 25	19 20 21 22 23 24 25
29 30 31	26 27 28	26 27 28 29 30 31

Friday
23

Saturday
24

Sunday
25

Notes:

Priority #5	Priority #6	Priority #7	Goal Focus:

February 26 - March 4   *2018*

Monday	
26	

Tuesday	
27	

Wednesday	
28	

Thursday	
1	

Priority #1	Priority #2	Priority #3	Priority #4

	JANUARY								FEBRUARY								MARCH					
M	T	W	T	F	S	S		M	T	W	T	F	S	S		M	T	W	T	F	S	S
1	2	3	4	5	6	7					1	2	3	4					1	2	3	4
8	9	10	11	12	13	14		5	6	7	8	9	10	11		5	6	7	8	9	10	11
15	16	17	18	19	20	21		12	13	14	15	16	17	18		12	13	14	15	16	17	18
22	23	24	25	26	27	28		19	20	21	22	23	24	25		19	20	21	22	23	24	25
29	30	31						26	27	28						26	27	28	29	30	31	

Friday
2

Saturday
3

Sunday
4

Notes:

Priority #5	Priority #6	Priority #7	Goal Focus:

Notes / Monthly Review

March

Birthdays / Anniversaries / Other Important Dates

Date	Event	Date	Event
_____	_____	_____	_____
_____	_____	_____	_____
_____	_____	_____	_____
_____	_____	_____	_____

Priority Focuses For the Month:

_____

_____

_____

_____

_____

Role Focuses For the Month:

_____

_____

_____

_____

_____

Goal Focuses For the Month:

_____

_____

_____

_____

_____

People I Need to Contact This Month

_____   _____

_____   _____

March   2018

Monday	Tuesday	Wednesday	Thursday
Notes:			1
5	6	7	8
12	13	14	15
19	20	21	22
26	27	28	29

Our greatest weakness lies in giving up. The most certain way to succeed is always to try just one more time. Thomas A. Edison

Friday	Saturday	Sunday	Notes/Focus
2	**3**	**4**	
9	**10**	**11**	
16	**17**	**18**	
23	**24**	**25**	
30	**31**	**Notes**	

PRG   PRG   PRG   PRG

Monday

5

Tuesday

6

Wednesday

7

Thursday

8

Priority #1	Priority #2	Priority #3	Priority #4

FEBRUARY	MARCH	APRIL
M T W T F S S	M T W T F S S	M T W T F S S
1 2 3 4	1 2 3 4	1
5 6 7 8 9 10 11	5 6 7 8 9 10 11	2 3 4 5 6 7 8
12 13 14 15 16 17 18	12 13 14 15 16 17 18	9 10 11 12 13 14 15
19 20 21 22 23 24 25	19 20 21 22 23 24 25	16 17 18 19 20 21 22
26 27 28	26 27 28 29 30 31	23 24 25 26 27 28 29
		30

Friday
9

Saturday
10

Sunday
11

Notes:

Priority #5	Priority #6	Priority #7	Goal Focus:

March 12 - 18   *2018*

Monday

12

Tuesday

13

Wednesday

14

Thursday

15

Priority #1	Priority #2	Priority #3	Priority #4

FEBRUARY	MARCH	APRIL
M T W T F S S	M T W T F S S	M T W T F S S
1 2 3 4	1 2 3 4	1
5 6 7 8 9 10 11	5 6 7 8 9 10 11	2 3 4 5 6 7 8
12 13 14 15 16 17 18	12 13 14 15 16 17 18	9 10 11 12 13 14 15
19 20 21 22 23 24 25	19 20 21 22 23 24 25	16 17 18 19 20 21 22
26 27 28	26 27 28 29 30 31	23 24 25 26 27 28 29
		30

Friday
16

_____

Saturday
17

_____

Sunday
18

_____

Notes:

_____

Priority #5	Priority #6	Priority #7	Goal Focus:

Monday	
19	

Tuesday	
20	

Wednesday	
21	

Thursday	
22	

Priority #1	Priority #2	Priority #3	Priority #4

FEBRUARY	MARCH	APRIL
M T W T F S S	M T W T F S S	M T W T F S S
1 2 3 4	1 2 3 4	1
5 6 7 8 9 10 11	5 6 7 8 9 10 11	2 3 4 5 6 7 8
12 13 14 15 16 17 18	12 13 14 15 16 17 18	9 10 11 12 13 14 15
19 20 21 22 23 24 25	19 20 21 22 23 24 25	16 17 18 19 20 21 22
26 27 28	26 27 28 29 30 31	23 24 25 26 27 28 29
		30

Friday
23

Saturday
24

Sunday
25

Notes:

Priority #5	Priority #6	Priority #7	Goal Focus:

March 26 - April 1   *2018*

Monday
26

Tuesday
27

Wednesday
28

Thursday
29

Priority #1	Priority #2	Priority #3	Priority #4

FEBRUARY	MARCH	APRIL
M T W T F S S	M T W T F S S	M T W T F S S
1 2 3 4	1 2 3 4	1
5 6 7 8 9 10 11	5 6 7 8 9 10 11	2 3 4 5 6 7 8
12 13 14 15 16 17 18	12 13 14 15 16 17 18	9 10 11 12 13 14 15
19 20 21 22 23 24 25	19 20 21 22 23 24 25	16 17 18 19 20 21 22
26 27 28	26 27 28 29 30 31	23 24 25 26 27 28 29
		30

Friday

30

Saturday

31

Sunday

1

Notes:

Priority #5	Priority #6	Priority #7	Goal Focus:

Notes / Monthly Review

April

Birthdays / Anniversaries / Other Important Dates

Date	Event	Date	Event
_____	_____	_____	_____
_____	_____	_____	_____
_____	_____	_____	_____
_____	_____	_____	_____

Priority Focuses For the Month:

_____

_____

_____

_____

_____

Role Focuses For the Month:

_____

_____

_____

_____

_____

Goal Focuses For the Month:

_____

_____

_____

_____

_____

People I Need to Contact This Month

_____   _____

_____   _____

_____   _____

April   2018

Monday	Tuesday	Wednesday	Thursday
Notes:			

2	3	4	5

9	10	11	12

16	17	18	19

23	24	25	26
30			

PRG   PRG   PRG   PRG

Friday	Saturday	Sunday	Notes/Focus
Notes:		1	
6	7	8	
13	14	15	
20	21	22	
27	28	29	

PRG   PRG   PRG   PRG

Monday

2

Tuesday

3

Wednesday

4

Thursday

5

Priority #1	Priority #2	Priority #3	Priority #4

	MARCH							APRIL							MAY					
M	T	W	T	F	S	S	M	T	W	T	F	S	S	M	T	W	T	F	S	S
			1	2	3	4							1		1	2	3	4	5	6
5	6	7	8	9	10	11	2	3	4	5	6	7	8	7	8	9	10	11	12	13
12	13	14	15	16	17	18	9	10	11	12	13	14	15	14	15	16	17	18	19	20
19	20	21	22	23	24	25	16	17	18	19	20	21	22	21	22	23	24	25	26	27
26	27	28	29	30	31		23	24	25	26	27	28	29	28	29	30	31			
							30													

Friday
6

Saturday
7

Sunday
8

Notes:

Priority #5	Priority #6	Priority #7	Goal Focus:

Monday	
9	

Tuesday	
10	

Wednesday	
11	

Thursday	
12	

Priority #1	Priority #2	Priority #3	Priority #4

MARCH								APRIL								MAY						
M	T	W	T	F	S	S		M	T	W	T	F	S	S		M	T	W	T	F	S	S
		1	2	3	4								1			1	2	3	4	5	6	
5	6	7	8	9	10	11		2	3	4	5	6	7	8		7	8	9	10	11	12	13
12	13	14	15	16	17	18		9	10	11	12	13	14	15		14	15	16	17	18	19	20
19	20	21	22	23	24	25		16	17	18	19	20	21	22		21	22	23	24	25	26	27
26	27	28	29	30	31			23	24	25	26	27	28	29		28	29	30	31			
								30														

Friday
13

Saturday
14

Sunday
15

Notes:

Priority #5	Priority #6	Priority #7	Goal Focus:

Monday

16

Tuesday

17

Wednesday

18

Thursday

19

Priority #1	Priority #2	Priority #3	Priority #4

	MARCH						
M	T	W	T	F	S	S
			1	2	3	4
5	6	7	8	9	10	11
12	13	14	15	16	17	18
19	20	21	22	23	24	25
26	27	28	29	30	31	

	APRIL						
M	T	W	T	F	S	S
						1
2	3	4	5	6	7	8
9	10	11	12	13	14	15
16	17	18	19	20	21	22
23	24	25	26	27	28	29
30						

	MAY						
M	T	W	T	F	S	S
	1	2	3	4	5	6
7	8	9	10	11	12	13
14	15	16	17	18	19	20
21	22	23	24	25	26	27
28	29	30	31			

Friday
20

Saturday
21

Sunday
22

Notes:

Priority #5	Priority #6	Priority #7	Goal Focus:

April 23 - 29   **2017**

Monday
23

Tuesday
24

Wednesday
25

Thursday
26

Priority #1	Priority #2	Priority #3	Priority #4

MARCH	APRIL	MAY
M T W T F S S	M T W T F S S	M T W T F S S
1 2 3 4	1	1 2 3 4 5 6
5 6 7 8 9 10 11	2 3 4 5 6 7 8	7 8 9 10 11 12 13
12 13 14 15 16 17 18	9 10 11 12 13 14 15	14 15 16 17 18 19 20
19 20 21 22 23 24 25	16 17 18 19 20 21 22	21 22 23 24 25 26 27
26 27 28 29 30 31	23 24 25 26 27 28 29	28 29 30 31
	30	

Friday
27

Saturday
28

Sunday
29

Notes:

Priority #5	Priority #6	Priority #7	Goal Focus:

Notes / Monthly Review

May

Birthdays / Anniversaries / Other Important Dates

Date	Event	Date	Event

Priority Focuses For the Month:

Role Focuses For the Month:

Goal Focuses For the Month:

People I Need to Contact This Month

May   *2018*

Monday	Tuesday	Wednesday	Thursday
Notes:	1	2	3
7	8	9	10
14	15	16	17
21	22	23	24
28	29	30	31

You cannot have a positive life and a negative mind.
Joyce Meyer

Friday	Saturday	Sunday	Notes/Focus
4	5	6	
11	12	13	
18	19	20	
25	26	27	

Notes:

Monday
30

Tuesday
1

Wednesday
2

Thursday
3

Priority #1	Priority #2	Priority #3	Priority #4

APRIL	MAY	JUNE

APRIL
M	T	W	T	F	S	S
						1
2	3	4	5	6	7	8
9	10	11	12	13	14	15
16	17	18	19	20	21	22
23	24	25	26	27	28	29
30						

MAY
M	T	W	T	F	S	S
1	2	3	4	5	6
7	8	9	10	11	12	13
14	15	16	17	18	19	20
21	22	23	24	25	26	27
28	29	30	31			

JUNE
M	T	W	T	F	S	S
				1	2	3
4	5	6	7	8	9	10
11	12	13	14	15	16	17
18	19	20	21	22	23	24
25	26	27	28	29	30	

Friday
4

Saturday
5

Sunday
6

Notes:

Priority #5	Priority #6	Priority #7	Goal Focus:

May 7 - 13   2018

Monday

7

Tuesday

8

Wednesday

9

Thursday

10

Priority #1	Priority #2	Priority #3	Priority #4

	APRIL								MAY								JUNE					
M	T	W	T	F	S	S		M	T	W	T	F	S	S		M	T	W	T	F	S	S
						1		1	2	3	4	5	6						1	2	3
2	3	4	5	6	7	8		7	8	9	10	11	12	13		4	5	6	7	8	9	10
9	10	11	12	13	14	15		14	15	16	17	18	19	20		11	12	13	14	15	16	17
16	17	18	19	20	21	22		21	22	23	24	25	26	27		18	19	20	21	22	23	24
23	24	25	26	27	28	29		28	29	30	31					25	26	27	28	29	30	
30																						

Friday
11

Saturday
12

Sunday
13

Notes:

Priority #5	Priority #6	Priority #7	Goal Focus:

May 14 - 20   2018

Monday
14

Tuesday
15

Wednesday
16

Thursday
17

Priority #1	Priority #2	Priority #3	Priority #4

APRIL	MAY	JUNE
M T W T F S S	M T W T F S S	M T W T F S S
1	1 2 3 4 5 6	1 2 3
2 3 4 5 6 7 8	7 8 9 10 11 12 13	4 5 6 7 8 9 10
9 10 11 12 13 14 15	14 15 16 17 18 19 20	11 12 13 14 15 16 17
16 17 18 19 20 21 22	21 22 23 24 25 26 27	18 19 20 21 22 23 24
23 24 25 26 27 28 29	28 29 30 31	25 26 27 28 29 30
30		

Friday
18

Saturday
19

Sunday
20

Notes:

Priority #5	Priority #6	Priority #7	Goal Focus:

May 21 - 27   *2018*

Monday
21

Tuesday
22

Wednesday
23

Thursday
24

Priority #1	Priority #2	Priority #3	Priority #4

APRIL	MAY	JUNE
M T W T F S S	M T W T F S S	M T W T F S S
1	1 2 3 4 5 6	1 2 3
2 3 4 5 6 7 8	7 8 9 10 11 12 13	4 5 6 7 8 9 10
9 10 11 12 13 14 15	14 15 16 17 18 19 20	11 12 13 14 15 16 17
16 17 18 19 20 21 22	21 22 23 24 25 26 27	18 19 20 21 22 23 24
23 24 25 26 27 28 29	28 29 30 31	25 26 27 28 29 30
30		

Friday

25

Saturday

26

Sunday

27

Notes:

Priority #5	Priority #6	Priority #7	Goal Focus:

Monday
28

Tuesday
29

Wednesday
30

Thursday
31

Priority #1	Priority #2	Priority #3	Priority #4

APRIL								MAY								JUNE						
M	T	W	T	F	S	S		M	T	W	T	F	S	S		M	T	W	T	F	S	S
						1		1	2	3	4	5	6						1	2	3	
2	3	4	5	6	7	8		7	8	9	10	11	12	13		4	5	6	7	8	9	10
9	10	11	12	13	14	15		14	15	16	17	18	19	20		11	12	13	14	15	16	17
16	17	18	19	20	21	22		21	22	23	24	25	26	27		18	19	20	21	22	23	24
23	24	25	26	27	28	29		28	29	30	31					25	26	27	28	29	30	
30																						

Friday

1

Saturday

2

Sunday

3

Notes:

Priority #5	Priority #6	Priority #7	Goal Focus:

Notes / Monthly Review

_____
_____
_____
_____
_____
_____
_____
_____
_____
_____
_____
_____
_____
_____
_____
_____
_____
_____
_____
_____
_____
_____
_____
_____
_____
_____
_____

June

Birthdays / Anniversaries / Other Important Dates

Date	Event	Date	Event
_____	_____	_____	_____
_____	_____	_____	_____
_____	_____	_____	_____
_____	_____	_____	_____

Priority Focuses For the Month:

_____

_____

_____

_____

_____

Role Focuses For the Month:

_____

_____

_____

_____

_____

Goal Focuses For the Month:

_____

_____

_____

_____

_____

People I Need to Contact This Month

_____   _____

_____   _____

June   2018

Monday	Tuesday	Wednesday	Thursday
Notes:			

4	5	6	7

11	12	13	14

18	19	20	21

25	26	27	28

Life is 10% what happens to you and 90% how you react to it. Charles R. Swindoll

Friday	Saturday	Sunday	Notes/Focus
1	**2**	**3**	
8	**9**	**10**	
15	**16**	**17**	
22	**23**	**24**	
29	**30**	*Notes:*	

June 4 - 10   2018

Monday

4

Tuesday

5

Wednesday

6

Thursday

7

Priority #1	Priority #2	Priority #3	Priority #4

	MAY							JUNE							JULY					
M	T	W	T	F	S	S	M	T	W	T	F	S	S	M	T	W	T	F	S	S
	1	2	3	4	5	6					1	2	3							1
7	8	9	10	11	12	13	4	5	6	7	8	9	10	2	3	4	5	6	7	8
14	15	16	17	18	19	20	11	12	13	14	15	16	17	9	10	11	12	13	14	15
21	22	23	24	25	26	27	18	19	20	21	22	23	24	16	17	18	19	20	21	22
28	29	30	31				25	26	27	28	29	30		23	24	25	26	27	28	29
														30	31					

Friday

8

Saturday

9

Sunday

10

Notes:

Priority #5	Priority #6	Priority #7	Goal Focus:

June 11 - 17   2018

Monday
11

Tuesday
12

Wednesday
13

Thursday
14

Priority #1	Priority #2	Priority #3	Priority #4

MAY	JUNE	JULY
M T W T F S S	M T W T F S S	M T W T F S S
1 2 3 4 5 6	1 2 3	1
7 8 9 10 11 12 13	4 5 6 7 8 9 10	2 3 4 5 6 7 8
14 15 16 17 18 19 20	11 12 13 14 15 16 17	9 10 11 12 13 14 15
21 22 23 24 25 26 27	18 19 20 21 22 23 24	16 17 18 19 20 21 22
28 29 30 31	25 26 27 28 29 30	23 24 25 26 27 28 29
		30 31

Friday
15

Saturday
16

Sunday
17

Notes:

Priority #5	Priority #6	Priority #7	Goal Focus:

Monday

18

Tuesday

19

Wednesday

20

Thursday

21

Priority #1	Priority #2	Priority #3	Priority #4

MAY								JUNE								JULY						
M	T	W	T	F	S	S		M	T	W	T	F	S	S		M	T	W	T	F	S	S
	1	2	3	4	5	6						1	2	3								1
7	8	9	10	11	12	13		4	5	6	7	8	9	10		2	3	4	5	6	7	8
14	15	16	17	18	19	20		11	12	13	14	15	16	17		9	10	11	12	13	14	15
21	22	23	24	25	26	27		18	19	20	21	22	23	24		16	17	18	19	20	21	22
28	29	30	31					25	26	27	28	29	30			23	24	25	26	27	28	29
																30	31					

Friday
22

Saturday
23

Sunday
24

Notes:

Priority #5	Priority #6	Priority #7	Goal Focus:

June 25 - July 1   *2018*

Monday

25

Tuesday

26

Wednesday

27

Thursday

28

Priority #1	Priority #2	Priority #3	Priority #4

MAY								JUNE								JULY						
M	T	W	T	F	S	S		M	T	W	T	F	S	S		M	T	W	T	F	S	S
	1	2	3	4	5	6						1	2	3								1
7	8	9	10	11	12	13		4	5	6	7	8	9	10		2	3	4	5	6	7	8
14	15	16	17	18	19	20		11	12	13	14	15	16	17		9	10	11	12	13	14	15
21	22	23	24	25	26	27		18	19	20	21	22	23	24		16	17	18	19	20	21	22
28	29	30	31					25	26	27	28	29	30			23	24	25	26	27	28	29
																30	31					

Friday
29

Saturday
30

Sunday
1

Notes:

Priority #5	Priority #6	Priority #7	Goal Focus:

Notes / Monthly Review

_____
_____
_____
_____
_____
_____
_____
_____
_____
_____
_____
_____
_____
_____
_____
_____
_____
_____
_____
_____
_____
_____
_____
_____
_____
_____
_____
_____
_____
_____

July

Birthdays / Anniversaries / Other Important Dates

Date	Event	Date	Event
_____	_____	_____	_____
_____	_____	_____	_____
_____	_____	_____	_____
_____	_____	_____	_____

Priority Focuses For the Month:

_____

_____

_____

_____

_____

Role Focuses For the Month:

_____

_____

_____

_____

_____

Goal Focuses For the Month:

_____

_____

_____

_____

_____

People I Need to Contact This Month

_____   _____

_____   _____

_____   _____

July 2018

Monday	Tuesday	Wednesday	Thursday
Notes:			

Monday	Tuesday	Wednesday	Thursday
2	3	4	5
9	10	11	12
16	17	18	19
23	24	25	26
30	31		

In every day, there are 1,440 minutes. That means we have 1,440 daily opportunities to make positive impact. Les Brown

Friday	Saturday	Sunday	Notes / Focus
Notes:		1	
6	7	8	
13	14	15	
20	21	22	
27	28	29	

PRG   PRG   PRG   PRG

Monday
2

Tuesday
3

Wednesday
4

Thursday
5

Priority #1	**Priority #2**	**Priority #3**	**Priority #4**

JUNE	JULY	AUGUST
M T W T F S S	M T W T F S S	M T W T F S S
1 2 3	1	1 2 3 4 5
4 5 6 7 8 9 10	2 3 4 5 6 7 8	6 7 8 9 10 11 12
11 12 13 14 15 16 17	9 10 11 12 13 14 15	13 14 15 16 17 18 19
18 19 20 21 22 23 24	16 17 18 19 20 21 22	20 21 22 23 24 25 26
25 26 27 28 29 30	23 24 25 26 27 28 29	27 28 29 30 31
	30 31	

Friday

6

Saturday

7

Sunday

8

Notes:

Priority #5	Priority #6	Priority #7	Goal Focus:

July 9 - 15   *2018*

Monday
9

Tuesday
10

Wednesday
11

Thursday
12

Priority #1	Priority #2	Priority #3	Priority #4

	JUNE							JULY							AUGUST					
M	T	W	T	F	S	S	M	T	W	T	F	S	S	M	T	W	T	F	S	S
				1	2	3							1			1	2	3	4	5
4	5	6	7	8	9	10	2	3	4	5	6	7	8	6	7	8	9	10	11	12
11	12	13	14	15	16	17	9	10	11	12	13	14	15	13	14	15	16	17	18	19
18	19	20	21	22	23	24	16	17	18	19	20	21	22	20	21	22	23	24	25	26
25	26	27	28	29	30		23	24	25	26	27	28	29	27	28	29	30	31		
							30	31												

Friday
13

Saturday
14

Sunday
15

Notes:

Priority #5	Priority #6	Priority #7	Goal Focus:

Monday
16

Tuesday
17

Wednesday
18

Thursday
19

Priority #1	Priority #2	Priority #3	Priority #4

JUNE						
M	T	W	T	F	S	S
				1	2	3
4	5	6	7	8	9	10
11	12	13	14	15	16	17
18	19	20	21	22	23	24
25	26	27	28	29	30	

JULY						
M	T	W	T	F	S	S
						1
2	3	4	5	6	7	8
9	10	11	12	13	14	15
16	17	18	19	20	21	22
23	24	25	26	27	28	29
30	31					

AUGUST						
M	T	W	T	F	S	S
	1	2	3	4	5	
6	7	8	9	10	11	12
13	14	15	16	17	18	19
20	21	22	23	24	25	26
27	28	29	30	31		

Friday
20

Saturday
21

Sunday
22

Notes:

Priority #5	Priority #6	Priority #7	Goal Focus:

Monday

23

Tuesday

24

Wednesday

25

Thursday

26

Priority #1	Priority #2	Priority #3	Priority #4

	JUNE								JULY								AUGUST					
M	T	W	T	F	S	S		M	T	W	T	F	S	S		M	T	W	T	F	S	S
				1	2	3								1			1	2	3	4	5
4	5	6	7	8	9	10		2	3	4	5	6	7	8		6	7	8	9	10	11	12
11	12	13	14	15	16	17		9	10	11	12	13	14	15		13	14	15	16	17	18	19
18	19	20	21	22	23	24		16	17	18	19	20	21	22		20	21	22	23	24	25	26
25	26	27	28	29	30			23	24	25	26	27	28	29		27	28	29	30	31		
								30	31													

Friday

27

Saturday

28

Sunday

29

Notes:

Priority #5	Priority #6	Priority #7	Goal Focus:

July 30 - August 5   *2018*

Monday
30

Tuesday
31

Wednesday
1

Thursday
2

Priority #1	Priority #2	Priority #3	Priority #4

	JUNE								JULY								AUGUST					
M	T	W	T	F	S	S		M	T	W	T	F	S	S		M	T	W	T	F	S	S
				1	2	3								1			1	2	3	4	5
4	5	6	7	8	9	10		2	3	4	5	6	7	8		6	7	8	9	10	11	12
11	12	13	14	15	16	17		9	10	11	12	13	14	15		13	14	15	16	17	18	19
18	19	20	21	22	23	24		16	17	18	19	20	21	22		20	21	22	23	24	25	26
25	26	27	28	29	30			23	24	25	26	27	28	29		27	28	29	30	31		
								30	31													

Friday

3

Saturday

4

Sunday

5

Notes:

Priority #5	Priority #6	Priority #7	Goal Focus:

Notes / Monthly Review

August

Birthdays / Anniversaries / Other Important Dates			
Date	Event	Date	Event
——	————	——	————
——	————	——	————
——	————	——	————
——	————	——	————

Priority Focuses For the Month:

_____

_____

_____

_____

_____

Role Focuses For the Month:

_____

_____

_____

_____

_____

Goal Focuses For the Month:

_____

_____

_____

_____

_____

People I Need to Contact This Month

_____ _____

_____ _____

_____ _____

August 2018

Monday	Tuesday	Wednesday	Thursday
Notes:		1	2
6	7	8	9
13	14	15	16
20	21	22	23
27	28	29	30

Friday	Saturday	Sunday	Notes / Focus
3	**4**	**5**	
10	**11**	**12**	
17	**18**	**19**	
24	**25**	**26**	
31	**Notes:**		

PRG   PRG   PRG   PRG

Monday

6

Tuesday

7

Wednesday

8

Thursday

9

Priority #1	Priority #2	Priority #3	Priority #4

	JULY								AUGUST								SEPTEMBER					
M	T	W	T	F	S	S		M	T	W	T	F	S	S		M	T	W	T	F	S	S
						1			1	2	3	4	5							1	2
2	3	4	5	6	7	8		6	7	8	9	10	11	12		3	4	5	6	7	8	9
9	10	11	12	13	14	15		13	14	15	16	17	18	19		10	11	12	13	14	15	16
16	17	18	19	20	21	22		20	21	22	23	24	25	26		17	18	19	20	21	22	23
23	24	25	26	27	28	29		27	28	29	30	31				24	25	26	27	28	29	30
30	31																					

Friday
10

Saturday
11

Sunday
12

Notes:

Priority #5	Priority #6	Priority #7	Goal Focus:

Monday

13

Tuesday

14

Wednesday

15

Thursday

16

Priority #1	Priority #2	Priority #3	Priority #4

JULY								AUGUST								SEPTEMBER						
M	T	W	T	F	S	S		M	T	W	T	F	S	S		M	T	W	T	F	S	S
						1		1	2	3	4	5								1	2
2	3	4	5	6	7	8		6	7	8	9	10	11	12		3	4	5	6	7	8	9
9	10	11	12	13	14	15		13	14	15	16	17	18	19		10	11	12	13	14	15	16
16	17	18	19	20	21	22		20	21	22	23	24	25	26		17	18	19	20	21	22	23
23	24	25	26	27	28	29		27	28	29	30	31				24	25	26	27	28	29	30
30	31																				

Friday
17

Saturday
18

Sunday
19

Notes:

Priority #5	Priority #6	Priority #7	Goal Focus:

Monday	
20	

Tuesday	
21	

Wednesday	
22	

Thursday	
23	

Priority #1	Priority #2	Priority #3	Priority #4

	JULY								AUGUST								SEPTEMBER					
M	T	W	T	F	S	S	M	T	W	T	F	S	S	M	T	W	T	F	S	S
						1		1	2	3	4	5							1	2
2	3	4	5	6	7	8	6	7	8	9	10	11	12	3	4	5	6	7	8	9
9	10	11	12	13	14	15	13	14	15	16	17	18	19	10	11	12	13	14	15	16
16	17	18	19	20	21	22	20	21	22	23	24	25	26	17	18	19	20	21	22	23
23	24	25	26	27	28	29	27	28	29	30	31			24	25	26	27	28	29	30
30	31																			

Friday
24

Saturday
25

Sunday
26

Notes:

Priority #5	Priority #6	Priority #7	Goal Focus:

August 27 - September 2   *2018*

Monday
27

Tuesday
28

Wednesday
29

Thursday
30

Priority #1	Priority #2	Priority #3	Priority #4

JULY							
M	T	W	T	F	S	S
						1
2	3	4	5	6	7	8
9	10	11	12	13	14	15
16	17	18	19	20	21	22
23	24	25	26	27	28	29
30	31					

AUGUST							
M	T	W	T	F	S	S
	1	2	3	4	5
6	7	8	9	10	11	12
13	14	15	16	17	18	19
20	21	22	23	24	25	26
27	28	29	30	31		

SEPTEMBER							
M	T	W	T	F	S	S
					1	2
3	4	5	6	7	8	9
10	11	12	13	14	15	16
17	18	19	20	21	22	23
24	25	26	27	28	29	30

Friday
31

Saturday
1

Sunday
2

Notes:

Priority #5	Priority #6	Priority #7	Goal Focus:

Notes / Monthly Review

September

Birthdays / Anniversaries / Other Important Dates

Date	Event	Date	Event
_____	_____	_____	_____
_____	_____	_____	_____
_____	_____	_____	_____
_____	_____	_____	_____

Priority Focuses For the Month:

_____

_____

_____

_____

_____

Role Focuses For the Month:

_____

_____

_____

_____

_____

Goal Focuses For the Month:

_____

_____

_____

_____

_____

People I Need to Contact This Month

_____ _____

_____ _____

_____ _____

September 2018

Monday	Tuesday	Wednesday	Thursday
Notes:			
3	**4**	**5**	**6**
10	**11**	**12**	**13**
17	**18**	**19**	**20**
24	**25**	**26**	**27**

The love of family and the admiration of friends is much more important than wealth and privilege. Charles Kuralt

Friday	Saturday	Sunday	Notes/Focus
Notes:	1	2	
7	8	9	
14	15	16	
21	22	23	
28	29	30	

PRG   PRG   PRG   PRG

Monday
3

Tuesday
4

Wednesday
5

Thursday
6

Priority #1	Priority #2	Priority #3	Priority #4

AUGUST	SEPTEMBER	OCTOBER

AUGUST

M	T	W	T	F	S	S
		1	2	3	4	5
6	7	8	9	10	11	12
13	14	15	16	17	18	19
20	21	22	23	24	25	26
27	28	29	30	31		

SEPTEMBER

M	T	W	T	F	S	S
					1	2
3	4	5	6	7	8	9
10	11	12	13	14	15	16
17	18	19	20	21	22	23
24	25	26	27	28	29	30

OCTOBER

M	T	W	T	F	S	S
1	2	3	4	5	6	7
8	9	10	11	12	13	14
15	16	17	18	19	20	21
22	23	24	25	26	27	28
29	30	31				

Friday
7

Saturday
8

Sunday
9

Notes:

Priority #5	Priority #6	Priority #7	Goal Focus:

September 10 - 16   2018

Monday
10

Tuesday
11

Wednesday
12

Thursday
13

Priority #1	Priority #2	Priority #3	Priority #4

M	T	W	T	F	S	S
		1	2	3	4	5
6	7	8	9	10	11	12
13	14	15	16	17	18	19
20	21	22	23	24	25	26
27	28	29	30	31		

M	T	W	T	F	S	S
					1	2
3	4	5	6	7	8	9
10	11	12	13	14	15	16
17	18	19	20	21	22	23
24	25	26	27	28	29	30

M	T	W	T	F	S	S
1	2	3	4	5	6	7
8	9	10	11	12	13	14
15	16	17	18	19	20	21
22	23	24	25	26	27	28
29	30	31				

Friday
14

Saturday
15

Sunday
16

Notes:

Priority #5	Priority #6	Priority #7	Goal Focus:

Monday
17

Tuesday
18

Wednesday
19

Thursday
20

Priority #1	Priority #2	Priority #3	Priority #4

AUGUST	SEPTEMBER	OCTOBER
M T W T F S S	M T W T F S S	M T W T F S S
1 2 3 4 5	1 2	1 2 3 4 5 6 7
6 7 8 9 10 11 12	3 4 5 6 7 8 9	8 9 10 11 12 13 14
13 14 15 16 17 18 19	10 11 12 13 14 15 16	15 16 17 18 19 20 21
20 21 22 23 24 25 26	17 18 19 20 21 22 23	22 23 24 25 26 27 28
27 28 29 30 31	24 25 26 27 28 29 30	29 30 31

Friday
21

Saturday
22

Sunday
23

Notes:

Priority #5	Priority #6	Priority #7	Goal Focus:

Monday
24

Tuesday
25

Wednesday
26

Thursday
27

Priority #1	Priority #2	Priority #3	Priority #4

	AUGUST							SEPTEMBER							OCTOBER					
M	T	W	T	F	S	S	M	T	W	T	F	S	S	M	T	W	T	F	S	S
	1	2	3	4	5						1	2		1	2	3	4	5	6	7
6	7	8	9	10	11	12	3	4	5	6	7	8	9	8	9	10	11	12	13	14
13	14	15	16	17	18	19	10	11	12	13	14	15	16	15	16	17	18	19	20	21
20	21	22	23	24	25	26	17	18	19	20	21	22	23	22	23	24	25	26	27	28
27	28	29	30	31			24	25	26	27	28	29	30	29	30	31				

Friday
28

Saturday
29

Sunday
30

Notes:

Priority #5	Priority #6	Priority #7	Goal Focus:

Notes / Monthly Review

October

Birthdays / Anniversaries / Other Important Dates

Date	Event	Date	Event
_____	_____	_____	_____
_____	_____	_____	_____
_____	_____	_____	_____
_____	_____	_____	_____

Priority Focuses For the Month:

_____

_____

_____

_____

_____

Role Focuses For the Month:

_____

_____

_____

_____

_____

Goal Focuses For the Month:

_____

_____

_____

_____

_____

People I Need to Contact This Month

_____   _____

_____   _____

_____   _____

October   2018

Monday	Tuesday	Wednesday	Thursday
1	2	3	4
8	9	10	11
15	16	17	18
22	23	24	25
29	30	31	Notes:

PRG   PRG   PRG   PRG

Don't fnnd fault, find a remedy.
Henry Ford

Friday	Saturday	Sunday	Notes/Focus
5	6	7	
12	13	14	
19	20	21	
26	27	28	
Notes:			

PRG   PRG   PRG   PRG

October 1 - 7   *2018*

Monday	
1	

Tuesday	
2	

Wednesday	
3	

Thursday	
4	

Priority #1	Priority #2	Priority #3	Priority #4

	SEPTEMBER						
M	T	W	T	F	S	S
				1	2
3	4	5	6	7	8	9
10	11	12	13	14	15	16
17	18	19	20	21	22	23
24	25	26	27	28	29	30

	OCTOBER						
M	T	W	T	F	S	S
1	2	3	4	5	6	7
8	9	10	11	12	13	14
15	16	17	18	19	20	21
22	23	24	25	26	27	28
29	30	31

	NOVEMBER						
M	T	W	T	F	S	S
			1	2	3	4
5	6	7	8	9	10	11
12	13	14	15	16	17	18
19	20	21	22	23	24	25
26	27	28	29	30

Friday
5

Saturday
6

Sunday
7

Notes:

Priority #5	Priority #6	Priority #7	Goal Focus:

Monday
8

Tuesday
9

Wednesday
10

Thursday
11

Priority #1	Priority #2	Priority #3	Priority #4

SEPTEMBER						
M	T	W	T	F	S	S
				1	2	
3	4	5	6	7	8	9
10	11	12	13	14	15	16
17	18	19	20	21	22	23
24	25	26	27	28	29	30

OCTOBER						
M	T	W	T	F	S	S
1	2	3	4	5	6	7
8	9	10	11	12	13	14
15	16	17	18	19	20	21
22	23	24	25	26	27	28
29	30	31				

NOVEMBER						
M	T	W	T	F	S	S
			1	2	3	4
5	6	7	8	9	10	11
12	13	14	15	16	17	18
19	20	21	22	23	24	25
26	27	28	29	30		

Friday
12

Saturday
13

Sunday
14

Notes:

Priority #5	Priority #6	Priority #7	Goal Focus:

October 15 - 21　　　　*2018*

Monday
15

Tuesday
16

Wednesday
17

Thursday
18

Priority #1	Priority #2	Priority #3	Priority #4

	SEPTEMBER							OCTOBER							NOVEMBER					
M	T	W	T	F	S	S	M	T	W	T	F	S	S	M	T	W	T	F	S	S
				1	2		1	2	3	4	5	6	7				1	2	3	4
3	4	5	6	7	8	9	8	9	10	11	12	13	14	5	6	7	8	9	10	11
10	11	12	13	14	15	16	15	16	17	18	19	20	21	12	13	14	15	16	17	18
17	18	19	20	21	22	23	22	23	24	25	26	27	28	19	20	21	22	23	24	25
24	25	26	27	28	29	30	29	30	31					26	27	28	29	30		

Friday
19

Saturday
20

Sunday
21

Notes:

Priority #5	Priority #6	Priority #7	Goal Focus:

October 22 - 28   2018

Monday

22

Tuesday

23

Wednesday

24

Thursday

25

Priority #1	Priority #2	Priority #3	Priority #4

SEPTEMBER	OCTOBER	NOVEMBER
M T W T F S S	M T W T F S S	M T W T F S S
1 2	1 2 3 4 5 6 7	1 2 3 4
3 4 5 6 7 8 9	8 9 10 11 12 13 14	5 6 7 8 9 10 11
10 11 12 13 14 15 16	15 16 17 18 19 20 21	12 13 14 15 16 17 18
17 18 19 20 21 22 23	22 23 24 25 26 27 28	19 20 21 22 23 24 25
24 25 26 27 28 29 30	29 30 31	26 27 28 29 30

Friday
26

Saturday
27

Sunday
28

Notes:

Priority #5	Priority #6	Priority #7	Goal Focus:

October 29 - November 4   *2018*

Monday
29

Tuesday
30

Wednesday
31

Thursday
1

Priority #1	Priority #2	Priority #3	Priority #4

SEPTEMBER	OCTOBER	NOVEMBER
M T W T F S S	M T W T F S S	M T W T F S S
1 2	1 2 3 4 5 6 7	1 2 3 4
3 4 5 6 7 8 9	8 9 10 11 12 13 14	5 6 7 8 9 10 11
10 11 12 13 14 15 16	15 16 17 18 19 20 21	12 13 14 15 16 17 18
17 18 19 20 21 22 23	22 23 24 25 26 27 28	19 20 21 22 23 24 25
24 25 26 27 28 29 30	29 30 31	26 27 28 29 30

Friday

2

Saturday

3

Sunday

4

Notes:

Priority #5	Priority #6	Priority #7	Goal Focus:

Notes / Monthly Review

November

Birthdays / Anniversaries / Other Important Dates

Date	Event	Date	Event
_____	_____	_____	_____
_____	_____	_____	_____
_____	_____	_____	_____

Priority Focuses For the Month:

_____

_____

_____

_____

_____

Role Focuses For the Month:

_____

_____

_____

_____

_____

Goal Focuses For the Month:

_____

_____

_____

_____

_____

People I Need to Contact This Month

_____   _____

_____   _____

November 2018

Monday	Tuesday	Wednesday	Thursday
Notes:			1
5	6	7	8
12	13	14	15
19	20	21	22
26	27	28	29

PRG　　　PRG　　　PRG　　　PRG

Education is the most powerful wepon which you can use to change the world.
Nelson Mandela

Friday	Saturday	Sunday	Notes/Focus
2	3	4	
9	10	11	
16	17	18	
23	24	25	
30	Notes:		

PRG   PRG   PRG   PRG

Monday

5

Tuesday

6

Wednesday

7

Thursday

8

Priority #1	Priority #2	Priority #3	Priority #4

	OCTOBER							NOVEMBER							DECEMBER					
M	T	W	T	F	S	S	M	T	W	T	F	S	S	M	T	W	T	F	S	S
1	2	3	4	5	6	7				1	2	3	4						1	2
8	9	10	11	12	13	14	5	6	7	8	9	10	11	3	4	5	6	7	8	9
15	16	17	18	19	20	21	12	13	14	15	16	17	18	10	11	12	13	14	15	16
22	23	24	25	26	27	28	19	20	21	22	23	24	25	17	18	19	20	21	22	23
29	30	31					26	27	28	29	30			24	25	26	27	28	29	30
														31						

Friday
9

Saturday
10

Sunday
11

Notes:

Priority #5	Priority #6	Priority #7	Goal Focus:

Monday	
12	

Tuesday	
13	

Wednesday	
14	

Thursday	
15	

Priority #1	Priority #2	Priority #3	Priority #4

OCTOBER								NOVEMBER								DECEMBER						
M	T	W	T	F	S	S		M	T	W	T	F	S	S		M	T	W	T	F	S	S
1	2	3	4	5	6	7					1	2	3	4							1	2
8	9	10	11	12	13	14		5	6	7	8	9	10	11		3	4	5	6	7	8	9
15	16	17	18	19	20	21		12	13	14	15	16	17	18		10	11	12	13	14	15	16
22	23	24	25	26	27	28		19	20	21	22	23	24	25		17	18	19	20	21	22	23
29	30	31						26	27	28	29	30				24	25	26	27	28	29	30
																31						

Friday
16

Saturday
17

Sunday
18

Notes:

Priority #5	Priority #6	Priority #7	Goal Focus:

Monday
19

Tuesday
20

Wednesday
21

Thursday
22

Priority #1	Priority #2	Priority #3	Priority #4

OCTOBER	NOVEMBER	DECEMBER
M T W T F S S	M T W T F S S	M T W T F S S
1 2 3 4 5 6 7	1 2 3 4	1 2
8 9 10 11 12 13 14	5 6 7 8 9 10 11	3 4 5 6 7 8 9
15 16 17 18 19 20 21	12 13 14 15 16 17 18	10 11 12 13 14 15 16
22 23 24 25 26 27 28	19 20 21 22 23 24 25	17 18 19 20 21 22 23
29 30 31	26 27 28 29 30	24 25 26 27 28 29 30
		31

Friday
23

Saturday
24

Sunday
25

Notes:

Priority #5	Priority #6	Priority #7	Goal Focus:

November 26 - December 2   *2018*

Monday
26

Tuesday
27

Wednesday
28

Thursday
29

Priority #1	Priority #2	Priority #3	Priority #4

OCTOBER	NOVEMBER	DECEMBER
M T W T F S S	M T W T F S S	M T W T F S S
1 2 3 4 5 6 7	1 2 3 4	1 2
8 9 10 11 12 13 14	5 6 7 8 9 10 11	3 4 5 6 7 8 9
15 16 17 18 19 20 21	12 13 14 15 16 17 18	10 11 12 13 14 15 16
22 23 24 25 26 27 28	19 20 21 22 23 24 25	17 18 19 20 21 22 23
29 30 31	26 27 28 29 30	24 25 26 27 28 29 30
		31

Friday

30

Saturday

1

Sunday

2

Notes:

Priority #5	Priority #6	Priority #7	Goal Focus:

Notes / Monthly Review

December

Birthdays / Anniversaries / Other Important Dates

Date	Event	Date	Event

Priority Focuses For the Month:

Role Focuses For the Month:

Goal Focuses For the Month:

People I Need to Contact This Month

December   2018

Monday	Tuesday	Wednesday	Thursday
Notes:			

3	4	5	6

10	11	12	13

17	18	19	20

24	25	26	27
31			

PRG   PRG   PRG   PRG

Friday	Saturday	Sunday	Notes/Focus
Notes:	**1**	**2**	
7	**8**	**9**	
14	**15**	**16**	
21	**22**	**23**	
28	**29**	**30**	

PRG   PRG   PRG   PRG

Monday

3

Tuesday

4

Wednesday

5

Thursday

6

Priority #1	Priority #2	Priority #3	Priority #4

NOVEMBER	DECEMBER	JANUARY
M T W T F S S	M T W T F S S	M T W T F S S
1 2 3 4	1 2	1 2 3 4 5 6
5 6 7 8 9 10 11	3 4 5 6 7 8 9	7 8 9 10 11 12 13
12 13 14 15 16 17 18	10 11 12 13 14 15 16	14 15 16 17 18 19 20
19 20 21 22 23 24 25	17 18 19 20 21 22 23	21 22 23 24 25 26 27
26 27 28 29 30	24 25 26 27 28 29 30	28 29 30 31
	31	

Friday

7

Saturday

8

Sunday

9

Notes:

Priority #5	Priority #6	Priority #7	Goal Focus:

Monday
10

Tuesday
11

Wednesday
12

Thursday
13

Priority #1	Priority #2	Priority #3	Priority #4

NOVEMBER								DECEMBER								JANUARY						
M	T	W	T	F	S	S		M	T	W	T	F	S	S		M	T	W	T	F	S	S
			1	2	3	4							1	2						1	5	6
5	6	7	8	9	10	11		3	4	5	6	7	8	9		7	8	9	10	11	12	13
12	13	14	15	16	17	18		10	11	12	13	14	15	16		14	15	16	17	18	19	20
19	20	21	22	23	24	25		17	18	19	20	21	22	23		21	22	23	24	25	26	27
26	27	28	29	30				24	25	26	27	28	29	30		28	29	30	31			
								31														

Friday

14

Saturday

15

Sunday

16

Notes:

Priority #5	Priority #6	Priority #7	Goal Focus:

Monday	
17	

Tuesday	
18	

Wednesday	
19	

Thursday	
20	

Priority #1	Priority #2	Priority #3	Priority #4

NOVEMBER	DECEMBER	JANUARY

NOVEMBER

M	T	W	T	F	S	S
		1	2	3	4
5	6	7	8	9	10	11
12	13	14	15	16	17	18
19	20	21	22	23	24	25
26	27	28	29	30		

DECEMBER

M	T	W	T	F	S	S
				1	2
3	4	5	6	7	8	9
10	11	12	13	14	15	16
17	18	19	20	21	22	23
24	25	26	27	28	29	30
31

JANUARY

M	T	W	T	F	S	S
1	2	3	4	5	6
7	8	9	10	11	12	13
14	15	16	17	18	19	20
21	22	23	24	25	26	27
28	29	30	31

Friday
21

Saturday
22

Sunday
23

Notes:

Priority #5	Priority #6	Priority #7	Goal Focus:

December 24 - 30   2018

Monday
24

Tuesday
25

Wednesday
26

Thursday
27

Priority #1	Priority #2	Priority #3	Priority #4

NOVEMBER								DECEMBER								JANUARY						
M	T	W	T	F	S	S		M	T	W	T	F	S	S		M	T	W	T	F	S	S
			1	2	3	4							1	2						1	5	6
5	6	7	8	9	10	11		3	4	5	6	7	8	9		7	8	9	10	11	12	13
12	13	14	15	16	17	18		10	11	12	13	14	15	16		14	15	16	17	18	19	20
19	20	21	22	23	24	25		17	18	19	20	21	22	23		21	22	23	24	25	26	27
26	27	28	29	30				24	25	26	27	28	29	30		28	29	30	31			
								31														

Friday
28

Saturday
29

Sunday
30

Notes:

Priority #5	Priority #6	Priority #7	Goal Focus:

Monday

31

Tuesday

1

Wednesday

2

Thursday

3

Priority #1	Priority #2	Priority #3	Priority #4

NOVEMBER	DECEMBER	JANUARY
M T W T F S S	M T W T F S S	M T W T F S S
1 2 3 4	1 2	1 2 3 4 5 6
5 6 7 8 9 10 11	3 4 5 6 7 8 9	7 8 9 10 11 12 13
12 13 14 15 16 17 18	10 11 12 13 14 15 16	14 15 16 17 18 19 20
19 20 21 22 23 24 25	17 18 19 20 21 22 23	21 22 23 24 25 26 27
26 27 28 29 30	24 25 26 27 28 29 30	28 29 30 31
	31	

Friday

4

Saturday

5

Sunday

6

Notes:

Priority #5	Priority #6	Priority #7	Goal Focus:

Notes / Monthly Review

Useful Information

Multiplication Table

×	0	1	2	3	4	5	6	7	8	9	10
0	0	0	0	0	0	0	0	0	0	0	0
1	0	1	2	3	4	5	6	7	8	9	10
2	0	2	4	6	8	10	12	14	16	18	20
3	0	3	6	9	12	15	18	21	24	27	30
4	0	4	8	12	16	20	24	28	32	36	40
5	0	5	10	15	20	25	30	35	40	45	50
6	0	6	12	18	24	30	36	42	48	54	60
7	0	7	14	21	28	35	42	49	56	63	70
8	0	8	16	24	32	40	48	56	64	72	80
9	0	9	18	27	36	45	54	63	72	81	90
10	0	10	20	30	40	50	60	70	80	90	100

6 When you multiply 6 by an even number, they both end in the same digit. Example: 6×2=12, 6×4=24, 6×6=36, etc.

9 the last digit goes 9, 8, 7, 6, … your hands can help! Example: to multiply 9 by 8, hold your 8th finger down, and count "7" and "2", the answer is 72

12 is 10× plus 2×

Fahrenheit to Celsius

F	C	F	C
5	-15	65	18
10	-12	70	21
15	-9.4	75	24
20	-6.7	80	27
25	-3.9	85	29
30	-1.1	90	32
35	1.7	95	35
40	4.4	100	38
45	7.2	105	41
50	10	110	43
55	13	115	46
60	16	120	49

$°C = (°F – 32)/1.8$

$°F = (°C × 1.8) + 32$

Roman Numerals Chart

1	I	21	XXI	41	XLI
2	II	22	XXII	42	XLII
3	III	23	XXIII	43	XLIII
4	IV	24	XXIV	44	XLIV
5	V	25	XXV	45	XLV
6	VI	26	XXVI	46	XLVI
7	VII	27	XXVII	47	XLVII
8	VIII	28	XXVIII	48	XLVIII
9	IX	29	XXIX	49	XLIX
10	X	30	XXX	50	L
11	XI	31	XXXI	100	C
12	XII	32	XXXII	500	D
13	XIII	33	XXXIII	1000	M
14	XIV	34	XXXIV		
15	XV	35	XXXV		
16	XVI	36	XXXVI		
17	XVII	37	XXXVII		
18	XVIII	38	XXXVIII		
19	XIX	39	XXXIX		
20	XX	40	XL		

Imperial Conversions

Length
1 mile = 1760 yards
1 mile = 8 furlong
1 furlong = 10 chains
1 chain = 4 rods
1 rod = 5 1/2 yards
1 yard = 3 feet
1 foot = 12 inches

Area
1 sq. mile = 640 acres
1 acre = 4840 sq. yard
1 sq. yard = 9 sq. feet
1 sq. foot = 144 sq. inches

Capacity
1 gal. = 4 quarts
1 quart = 2 pints
1 pint = 4 gills
1 pint = 34.6774 inchs3
1 gill = 5 fl. oz.
1 fl. oz. = 8 fl. drachms
1 US gal. = 0.8327 gal
1 US pint = 0.8327 pint
1 US pint = 16 fl. oz.
1 yard3 = 27 feet3
1 foot3 = 1728 inches3

Weight
1 ton = 20 cwt
1 ton = 2240 lb.
1 ton = 1.12 US ton
1 cwt = 4 quarters
1 quarter = 2 stone.
1 stone = 14 lb.
1 lb. = 16 oz.
1 oz. = 16 drams
1 oz. = 437.5 grains
1 US ton = 2000 lb.

Unit Conversions

Unit:	Equals:	Equals:
1 tsp.	1/6 fl. oz.	1/3 Tbsp.
1 Tbsp.	½ fl. oz.	3 tsp.
1/8 cup	1 fl. oz.	2 Tbsp.
¼ cup	2 fl. oz.	4 Tbsp.
1/3 cup	2¾ fl. oz.	¼ cup plus 4 tsp.
½ cup	4 fl. oz.	8 Tbsp.
1 cup	8 fl. oz.	½ pint
1 pint	16 fl. oz.	2 cups
1 quart	32 fl. oz.	2 pints
1 liter	34 fl. oz.	1 quart plus ¼ cup
1 gallon	128 fl. oz.	4 quarts

Formulas

Angles
Sum of Interior Angles of Polygon = (n-2)(180)
n = number of sides of a polygon
Central Angle = 2(Inscribed Angle)

Area
Square: $A = a2$
Rectangle: $A = lw$
Parallelogram: $A = bh$
Trapezoid: $A = .5(a+c)h$, where a and c are the lengths of the parallel sides

Circles
$π = pi = 3.1415$
Area: $A = πr2$
Circumference: $C = 2πr$
Central Angle = 2(Inscribed Angle)
Area of Sector = $(x/360)πr2$

Volume
Cube: $V = a3$ where a is the length of a side
Rectangular Solid: $V = hwl$
Cylinder: $V = πr2h$

Perimeter
Square: $P = 4l$
Rectangle: $P = 2w + 2l$
Parallelogram: $P = 2b + 2a$, where a and b are the lengths of the non-parallel sides
Circle: $P = 2πr$

Triangles
Area: $A = .5bh$
Pythagorean Theorem: $A2 + B2 = C2$
where A = one leg, B = the other leg,
C = hypotenuse

Order of Operations
P - Parentheses
E - Exponents
M - Multiplication
D - Division
A - Addition
S - Subtraction

Other
$x3 = x*x*x$
Distance = Rate*Time

States and Capitals

State	Capital	State	Capital
Alabama	Montgomery	Montana	Helena
Alaska	Juneau	Nebraska	Lincoln
Arizona	Phoenix	Nevada	Carson City
Arkansas	Little Rock	New Hampshire	Concord
California	Sacramento	New Jersey	Trenton
Colorado	Denver	New Mexico	Santa Fe
Connecticut	Hartford	New York	Albany
Delaware	Dover	North Carolina	Raleigh
Florida	Tallahassee	North Dakota	Bismarck
Georgia	Atlanta	Ohio	Columbus
Hawaii	Honolulu	Oklahoma	Oklahoma City
Idaho	Boise	Oregon	Salem
Illinois	Springfield	Pennsylvania	Harrisburg
Indiana	Indianapolis	Rhode Island	Providence
Iowa	Des Moines	South Carolina	Columbia
Kansas	Topeka	South Dakota	Pierre
Kentucky	Frankfort	Tennessee	Nashville
Louisiana	Baton Rouge	Texas	Austin
Maine	Augusta	Utah	Salt Lake City
Maryland	Annapolis	Vermont	Montpelier
Massachusetts	Boston	Virginia	Richmond
Michigan	Lansing	Washington	Olympia
Minnesota	St. Paul	West Virginia	Charleston
Mississippi	Jackson	Wisconsin	Madison
Missouri	Jefferson City	Wyoming	Cheyenne

Presidents of the United States

#	President	#	President
1	Washington, George	23	Harrison, Benjamin
2	Adams, John	24	Cleveland, Grover
3	Jefferson, Thomas	25	McKinley, William
4	Madison, James	26	Roosevelt, Theodore
5	Monroe, James	27	Taft, William Howard
6	Adams, John Quincy	28	Wilson, Woodrow
7	Jackson, Andrew	29	Harding, Warren Gamaliel
8	Van Buren, Martin	30	Coolidge, Calvin
9	Harrison, William Henry	31	Hoover, Herbert Clark
10	Tyler, John	32	Roosevelt, Franklin Delano
11	Polk, James Knox	33	Truman, Harry
12	Taylor, Zachary	34	Eisenhower, Dwight David
13	Fillmore, Millard	35	Kennedy, John Fitzgerald
14	Pierce, Franklin	36	Johnson, Lyndon Baines
15	Buchanan, James	37	Nixon, Richard Milhous
16	Lincoln, Abraham	38	Ford, Gerald Rudolph
17	Johnson, Andrew	39	Carter, James Earl Jr.
18	Grant, Ulysses S.	40	Reagan, Ronald Wilson
19	Hayes, Rutherford Birchard	41	Bush, George Herbert Walker
20	Garfield, James Abram	42	Clinton, William Jefferson
21	Arthur, Chester Alan	43	Bush, George Walker
22	Cleveland, Grover	44	Obama, Barack Hussein
		45	Trump, Donald J.

Future Planning

January 2019

Date:	Event:	Date:	Event:

February 2019

Date:	Event:	Date:	Event:

March 2019

Date:	Event:	Date:	Event:

April 2019

Date:	Event:	Date:	Event:

May 2019

Date:	Event:	Date:	Event:

June 2019

Date:	Event:	Date:	Event:

July 2019

Date:	Event:	Date:	Event:

August 2019

Date:	Event:	Date:	Event:

September 2019

Date:	Event:	Date:	Event:

October 2019

Date:	Event:	Date:	Event:

November 2019

Date:	Event:	Date:	Event:

December 2019

Date:	Event:	Date:	Event:

January 2020

Date:	Event:

February 2020

Date:	Event:

March 2020

Date:	Event:

April 2020

Date:	Event:

May 2020

Date:	Event:

June 2020

Date:	Event:

July 2020

Date:	Event:

August 2020

Date:	Event:

September 2020

Date:	Event:

October 2020

Date:	Event:

November 2020

Date:	Event:

December 2020

Date:	Event:

> *The will to win, the desire to succeed, the urge to reach your full potential... these are the keys that will unlock the door to personal excellence.*
> **Confucius**

Medical Information

Primary Physician

		Visit Date:	Reason / Outcome
Doctor:			
Phone Number:			
Fax Number:			
Address:			
Insurance Number:			

Eye Doctor

		Visit Date:	Reason / Outcome
Doctor:			
Phone Number:			
Fax Number:			
Address			
Insurance Number:			

Dentist

		Visit Date:	Reason / Outcome
Doctor:			
Phone Number:			
Fax Number:			
Address:			
Insurance Number:			

Other:

		Visit Date:	Reason / Outcome
Doctor:			
Phone Number:			
Fax Number:			
Address:			
Insurance Number:			

Blood Type:

Social Security #:

Driver License #:

Medication	Amount	Time

Personal Profile Sheet (Family and Friends)

Name: _____

Address: _____ **Physician:** _____
_____ Phone #: _____
_____ Fax #: _____
Home #: _____ **Eye Doctor:** _____
Cell #: _____ Phone #: _____
Fax #: _____ Fax #: _____
Birthday: _____ **Dentist:** _____
Anniversary: _____ Phone #: _____
Social Sec. #: _____ Fax #: _____
Other: _____ Insurance #: _____

Name: _____

Address: _____ **Physician:** _____
_____ Phone #: _____
_____ Fax #: _____
Home #: _____ **Eye Doctor:** _____
Cell #: _____ Phone #: _____
Fax #: _____ Fax #: _____
Birthday: _____ **Dentist:** _____
Anniversary: _____ Phone #: _____
Social Sec. #: _____ Fax #: _____
Other: _____ Insurance #: _____

Name: _____

Address: _____ **Physician:** _____
_____ Phone #: _____
_____ Fax #: _____
Home #: _____ **Eye Doctor:** _____
Cell #: _____ Phone #: _____
Fax #: _____ Fax #: _____
Birthday: _____ **Dentist:** _____
Anniversary: _____ Phone #: _____
Social Sec. #: _____ Fax #: _____
Other: _____ Insurance #: _____

Name: _____

Address: _____ **Physician:** _____
_____ Phone #: _____
_____ Fax #: _____
Home #: _____ **Eye Doctor:** _____
Cell #: _____ Phone #: _____
Fax #: _____ Fax #: _____
Birthday: _____ **Dentist:** _____
Anniversary: _____ Phone #: _____
Social Sec. #: _____ Fax #: _____
Other: _____ Insurance #: _____

Name:		
Address:		**Physician:**
		Phone #:
		Fax #:
Home #:		**Eye Doctor:**
Cell #:		Phone #:
Fax #:		Fax #:
Birthday:		**Dentist:**
Anniversary:		Phone #:
Social Sec. #:		Fax #:
Other:		Insurance #:

Name:		
Address:		**Physician:**
		Phone #:
		Fax #:
Home #:		**Eye Doctor:**
Cell #:		Phone #:
Fax #:		Fax #:
Birthday:		**Dentist:**
Anniversary:		Phone #:
Social Sec. #:		Fax #:
Other:		Insurance #:

Name:		
Address:		**Physician:**
		Phone #:
		Fax #:
Home #:		**Eye Doctor:**
Cell #:		Phone #:
Fax #:		Fax #:
Birthday:		**Dentist:**
Anniversary:		Phone #:
Social Sec. #:		Fax #:
Other:		Insurance #:

Name:		
Address:		**Physician:**
		Phone #:
		Fax #:
Home #:		**Eye Doctor:**
Cell #:		Phone #:
Fax #:		Fax #:
Birthday:		**Dentist:**
Anniversary:		Phone #:
Social Sec. #:		Fax #:
Other:		Insurance #:

If opportunity doesn't knock, build a door.

Milton Berle

Web Log

Website:	Notes:
Address:	
Username:	
Password:	

Website:	Notes:
Address:	
Username:	
Password:	

Website:	Notes:
Address:	
Username:	
Password:	

Website:	Notes:
Address:	
Username:	
Password:	

Website:	Notes:
Address:	
Username:	
Password:	

Website:	Notes:
Address:	
Username:	
Password:	

Website:	Notes:
Address:	
Username:	
Password:	

Website:	Notes:
Address:	
Username:	
Password:	

Website:	Notes:
Address:	
Username:	
Password:	

* Helpful Hint - Use a code when writing down passwords. For example: if your password is MiamiDolphins21, write down MD# something only you would know.

Website:	Notes:
Address:	
Username:	
Password:	

Website:	Notes:
Address:	
Username:	
Password:	

Website:	Notes:
Address:	
Username:	
Password:	

Website:	Notes:
Address:	
Username:	
Password:	

Website:	Notes:
Address:	
Username:	
Password:	

Website:	Notes:
Address:	
Username:	
Password:	

Website:	Notes:
Address:	
Username:	
Password:	

Website:	Notes:
Address:	
Username:	
Password:	

Website:	Notes:
Address:	
Username:	
Password:	

Website:	Notes:
Address:	
Username:	
Password:	

Contacts / Resource File

Name:	Home #:
Address:	Work #:
	Cell #:
E-Mail:	Fax #:
Connection:	Other:

Name:	Home #:
Address:	Work #:
	Cell #:
E-Mail:	Fax #:
Connection:	Other:

Name:	Home #:
Address:	Work #:
	Cell #:
E-Mail:	Fax #:
Connection:	Other:

Name:	Home #:
Address:	Work #:
	Cell #:
E-Mail:	Fax #:
Connection:	Other:

Name:	Home #:
Address:	Work #:
	Cell #:
E-Mail:	Fax #:
Connection:	Other:

Name:	Home #:
Address:	Work #:
	Cell #:
E-Mail:	Fax #:
Connection:	Other:

Name:	Home #:
Address:	Work #:
	Cell #:
E-Mail:	Fax #:
Connection:	Other:

Name:	Home #:
Address:	Work #:
	Cell #:
E-Mail:	Fax #:
Connection:	Other:

* Helpful Hint - Write down connections for people you place in your contacts such as "met at town meeting" or "co-worker's associate." That way you will remember how you know that person. If you don't have constant contact with that person, you may forget how you know them.

Name:	Home #:
Address:	Work #:
	Cell #:
E-Mail:	Fax #:
Connection:	Other:

Name:	Home #:
Address:	Work #:
	Cell #:
E-Mail:	Fax #:
Connection:	Other:

Name:	Home #:
Address:	Work #:
	Cell #:
E-Mail:	Fax #:
Connection:	Other:

Name:	Home #:
Address:	Work #:
	Cell #:
E-Mail:	Fax #:
Connection:	Other:

Name:	Home #:
Address:	Work #:
	Cell #:
E-Mail:	Fax #:
Connection:	Other:

Name:	Home #:
Address:	Work #:
	Cell #:
E-Mail:	Fax #:
Connection:	Other:

Name:	Home #:
Address:	Work #:
	Cell #:
E-Mail:	Fax #:
Connection:	Other:

Name:	Home #:
Address:	Work #:
	Cell #:
E-Mail:	Fax #:
Connection:	Other:

Journal

Date:	

Date:	

Date:	

Date:	

Date:	

Date:	

Date:	

Date:	

Date:	

Date:	

Date:	

Date:	

Goal Sheet

Priority:	Role:

Start Date:	Type of Goal: Daily Short Long	Completion Date:

Goal:

A)   <u>What do you need to do to obtain this goal? What needs to get done?</u>

1 _____ 7 _____
2 _____ 8 _____
3 _____ 9 _____
4 _____ 10 _____
5 _____ 11 _____
6 _____ 12 _____

B)   <u>Steps / Timeline of Events</u>

1 _____ 7 _____
2 _____ 8 _____
3 _____ 9 _____
4 _____ 10 _____
5 _____ 11 _____
6 _____ 12 _____

C)   <u>People Who Can Help</u>

1 _____ 5 _____
2 _____ 6 _____
3 _____ 7 _____
4 _____ 8 _____

D)   <u>Positive BAS</u>

1 _____
2 _____
3 _____
4 _____

E)   <u>Negative BAS</u>

1 _____
2 _____
3 _____
4 _____

F)   <u>Notes / Follow-Up</u>

_____
_____
_____
_____
_____
_____

G)   <u>Next Steps</u>

_____
_____
_____
_____
_____
_____

Goal Sheet

| Priority: | | Role: | |

| Start Date: | Type of Goal:
Daily   Short   Long | Completion Date: |

| **Goal:** | |

A)   What do you need to do to obtain this goal? What needs to get done?

1	_____	7	_____
2	_____	8	_____
3	_____	9	_____
4	_____	10	_____
5	_____	11	_____
6	_____	12	_____

B)   Steps / Timeline of Events

1	_____	7	_____
2	_____	8	_____
3	_____	9	_____
4	_____	10	_____
5	_____	11	_____
6	_____	12	_____

C)   People Who Can Help

1	_____	5	_____
2	_____	6	_____
3	_____	7	_____
4	_____	8	_____

D)   Positive BAS

1 _____
2 _____
3 _____
4 _____

E)   Negative BAS

1 _____
2 _____
3 _____
4 _____

F)   Notes / Follow-Up

_____
_____
_____
_____
_____
_____
_____

G)   Next Steps

_____
_____
_____
_____
_____
_____
_____

Goal Sheet

Priority:		Role:

Start Date:	Type of Goal: Daily Short Long	Completion Date:

Goal:

A)   <u>What do you need to do to obtain this goal? What needs to get done?</u>

1 _____   7 _____
2 _____   8 _____
3 _____   9 _____
4 _____   10 _____
5 _____   11 _____
6 _____   12 _____

B)   <u>Steps / Timeline of Events</u>

1 _____   7 _____
2 _____   8 _____
3 _____   9 _____
4 _____   10 _____
5 _____   11 _____
6 _____   12 _____

C)   <u>People Who Can Help</u>

1 _____   5 _____
2 _____   6 _____
3 _____   7 _____
4 _____   8 _____

D)   <u>Positive BAS</u>   **E)**   <u>Negative BAS</u>

1 _____   1 _____
2 _____   2 _____
3 _____   3 _____
4 _____   4 _____

F)   <u>Notes / Follow-Up</u>   **G)**   <u>Next Steps</u>

_____   _____
_____   _____
_____   _____
_____   _____
_____   _____
_____   _____

Goal Sheet

| Priority: | | Role: | |

| Start Date: | Type of Goal:
Daily   Short   Long | Completion Date: |

| **Goal:** | |

A)   __What do you need to do to obtain this goal? What needs to get done?__

- [ ] 1 _____
- [ ] 2 _____
- [ ] 3 _____
- [ ] 4 _____
- [ ] 5 _____
- [ ] 6 _____

- [ ] 7 _____
- [ ] 8 _____
- [ ] 9 _____
- [ ] 10 _____
- [ ] 11 _____
- [ ] 12 _____

B)   __Steps / Timeline of Events__

- [ ] 1 _____
- [ ] 2 _____
- [ ] 3 _____
- [ ] 4 _____
- [ ] 5 _____
- [ ] 6 _____

- [ ] 7 _____
- [ ] 8 _____
- [ ] 9 _____
- [ ] 10 _____
- [ ] 11 _____
- [ ] 12 _____

C)   __People Who Can Help__

- [ ] 1 _____
- [ ] 2 _____
- [ ] 3 _____
- [ ] 4 _____

- [ ] 5 _____
- [ ] 6 _____
- [ ] 7 _____
- [ ] 8 _____

D)   __Positive BAS__

1 _____
2 _____
3 _____
4 _____

E)   __Negative BAS__

1 _____
2 _____
3 _____
4 _____

F)   __Notes / Follow-Up__

_____
_____
_____
_____
_____
_____

G)   __Next Steps__

_____
_____
_____
_____
_____
_____

Goal Sheet

Priority:	Role:

Start Date:	Type of Goal: Daily Short Long	Completion Date:

Goal:	

A)   <u>What do you need to do to obtain this goal? What needs to get done?</u>

1	_____	7	_____
2	_____	8	_____
3	_____	9	_____
4	_____	10	_____
5	_____	11	_____
6	_____	12	_____

B)   <u>Steps / Timeline of Events</u>

1	_____	7	_____
2	_____	8	_____
3	_____	9	_____
4	_____	10	_____
5	_____	11	_____
6	_____	12	_____

C)   <u>People Who Can Help</u>

1	_____	5	_____
2	_____	6	_____
3	_____	7	_____
4	_____	8	_____

D)   <u>Positive BAS</u>   **E)**   <u>Negative BAS</u>

1	_____	1	_____
2	_____	2	_____
3	_____	3	_____
4	_____	4	_____

F)   <u>Notes / Follow-Up</u>   **G)**   <u>Next Steps</u>

Goal Sheet

Priority:	Role:

Start Date:	Type of Goal: Daily Short Long	Completion Date:

Goal:	

A)   <u>What do you need to do to obtain this goal? What needs to get done?</u>

- ☐ 1 _____
- ☐ 2 _____
- ☐ 3 _____
- ☐ 4 _____
- ☐ 5 _____
- ☐ 6 _____
- ☐ 7 _____
- ☐ 8 _____
- ☐ 9 _____
- ☐ 10 _____
- ☐ 11 _____
- ☐ 12 _____

B)   <u>Steps / Timeline of Events</u>

- ☐ 1 _____
- ☐ 2 _____
- ☐ 3 _____
- ☐ 4 _____
- ☐ 5 _____
- ☐ 6 _____
- ☐ 7 _____
- ☐ 8 _____
- ☐ 9 _____
- ☐ 10 _____
- ☐ 11 _____
- ☐ 12 _____

C)   <u>People Who Can Help</u>

- ☐ 1 _____
- ☐ 2 _____
- ☐ 3 _____
- ☐ 4 _____
- ☐ 5 _____
- ☐ 6 _____
- ☐ 7 _____
- ☐ 8 _____

D)   <u>Positive BAS</u>

- 1 _____
- 2 _____
- 3 _____
- 4 _____

E)   <u>Negative BAS</u>

- 1 _____
- 2 _____
- 3 _____
- 4 _____

F)   <u>Notes / Follow-Up</u>

_____
_____
_____
_____
_____
_____

G)   <u>Next Steps</u>

_____
_____
_____
_____
_____
_____

Goal Sheet

Priority: Role:

Start Date: Type of Goal: Completion Date:

                        Daily   Short   Long

Goal:

A)   <u>What do you need to do to obtain this goal? What needs to get done?</u>

1   7
2   8
3   9
4   10
5   11
6   12

B)   <u>Steps / Timeline of Events</u>

1   7
2   8
3   9
4   10
5   11
6   12

C)   <u>People Who Can Help</u>

1   5
2   6
3   7
4   8

D)   **Positive BAS**   **E)**   **Negative BAS**

1   1
2   2
3   3
4   4

F)   **Notes / Follow-Up**   **G)**   **Next Steps**

Goal Sheet

Priority:	Role:

Start Date:	Type of Goal: Daily Short Long	Completion Date:

Goal:

A)   What do you need to do to obtain this goal? What needs to get done?

1	_____	7	_____
2	_____	8	_____
3	_____	9	_____
4	_____	10	_____
5	_____	11	_____
6	_____	12	_____

B)   Steps / Timeline of Events

1	_____	7	_____
2	_____	8	_____
3	_____	9	_____
4	_____	10	_____
5	_____	11	_____
6	_____	12	_____

C)   People Who Can Help

1	_____	5	_____
2	_____	6	_____
3	_____	7	_____
4	_____	8	_____

D)   Positive BAS   E)   Negative BAS

1	_____	1	_____
2	_____	2	_____
3	_____	3	_____
4	_____	4	_____

F)   Notes / Follow-Up   G)   Next Steps

Goal Sheet

Priority:		Role:

Start Date:	Type of Goal: Daily Short Long	Completion Date:

Goal:	

A)   What do you need to do to obtain this goal? What needs to get done?

☐ 1 _____	☐ 7 _____
☐ 2 _____	☐ 8 _____
☐ 3 _____	☐ 9 _____
☐ 4 _____	☐ 10 _____
☐ 5 _____	☐ 11 _____
☐ 6 _____	☐ 12 _____

B)   Steps / Timeline of Events

☐ 1 _____	☐ 7 _____
☐ 2 _____	☐ 8 _____
☐ 3 _____	☐ 9 _____
☐ 4 _____	☐ 10 _____
☐ 5 _____	☐ 11 _____
☐ 6 _____	☐ 12 _____

C)   People Who Can Help

☐ 1 _____	☐ 5 _____
☐ 2 _____	☐ 6 _____
☐ 3 _____	☐ 7 _____
☐ 4 _____	☐ 8 _____

D)   Positive BAS

1 _____
2 _____
3 _____
4 _____

E)   Negative BAS

1 _____
2 _____
3 _____
4 _____

F)   Notes / Follow-Up

_____
_____
_____
_____
_____
_____

G)   Next Steps

_____
_____
_____
_____
_____
_____

Goal Sheet

Priority:		Role:

Start Date:	Type of Goal: Daily Short Long	Completion Date:

Goal:

A)   <u>What do you need to do to obtain this goal? What needs to get done?</u>

1 _____	7 _____
2 _____	8 _____
3 _____	9 _____
4 _____	10 _____
5 _____	11 _____
6 _____	12 _____

B)   <u>Steps / Timeline of Events</u>

1 _____	7 _____
2 _____	8 _____
3 _____	9 _____
4 _____	10 _____
5 _____	11 _____
6 _____	12 _____

C)   <u>People Who Can Help</u>

1 _____	5 _____
2 _____	6 _____
3 _____	7 _____
4 _____	8 _____

D)   <u>Positive BAS</u>   **E)**   <u>Negative BAS</u>

1 _____	1 _____
2 _____	2 _____
3 _____	3 _____
4 _____	4 _____

F)   <u>Notes / Follow-Up</u>   **G)**   <u>Next Steps</u>

Goal Sheet

Priority: _____ | Role: _____

| Start Date: | Type of Goal:
Daily   Short   Long | Completion Date: |

Goal: _____

A)   What do you need to do to obtain this goal? What needs to get done?

1 _____   7 _____
2 _____   8 _____
3 _____   9 _____
4 _____   10 _____
5 _____   11 _____
6 _____   12 _____

B)   Steps / Timeline of Events

1 _____   7 _____
2 _____   8 _____
3 _____   9 _____
4 _____   10 _____
5 _____   11 _____
6 _____   12 _____

C)   People Who Can Help

1 _____   5 _____
2 _____   6 _____
3 _____   7 _____
4 _____   8 _____

D)   Positive BAS   E)   Negative BAS

1 _____   1 _____
2 _____   2 _____
3 _____   3 _____
4 _____   4 _____

F)   Notes / Follow-Up   G)   Next Steps

_____   _____
_____   _____
_____   _____
_____   _____
_____   _____
_____   _____

Goal Sheet

| Priority: | | Role: | |

| Start Date: | Type of Goal:
Daily   Short   Long | Completion Date: |

| **Goal:** | |

A)   What do you need to do to obtain this goal? What needs to get done?

1 _____ 7 _____
2 _____ 8 _____
3 _____ 9 _____
4 _____ 10 _____
5 _____ 11 _____
6 _____ 12 _____

B)   Steps / Timeline of Events

1 _____ 7 _____
2 _____ 8 _____
3 _____ 9 _____
4 _____ 10 _____
5 _____ 11 _____
6 _____ 12 _____

C)   People Who Can Help

1 _____ 5 _____
2 _____ 6 _____
3 _____ 7 _____
4 _____ 8 _____

D)   Positive BAS   E)   Negative BAS

1 _____ 1 _____
2 _____ 2 _____
3 _____ 3 _____
4 _____ 4 _____

F)   Notes / Follow-Up   G)   Next Steps

_____ _____
_____ _____
_____ _____
_____ _____
_____ _____
_____ _____

Goal Sheet

Priority:		Role:

Start Date:	Type of Goal: Daily Short Long	Completion Date:

Goal: _____

A)   What do you need to do to obtain this goal? What needs to get done?

1	_____	7	_____
2		8	
3		9	
4		10	
5		11	
6		12	

B)   Steps / Timeline of Events

1	_____	7	_____
2		8	
3		9	
4		10	
5		11	
6		12	

C)   People Who Can Help

1	_____	5	_____
2		6	
3		7	
4		8	

D)   Positive BAS   E)   Negative BAS

1	_____	1	_____
2		2	
3		3	
4		4	

F)   Notes / Follow-Up   G)   Next Steps

_____

Goal Sheet

Priority:		Role:

Start Date:	Type of Goal: Daily Short Long	Completion Date:

Goal: _____

A)   What do you need to do to obtain this goal? What needs to get done?

☐	1	_____	☐	7	_____
☐	2	_____	☐	8	_____
☐	3	_____	☐	9	_____
☐	4	_____	☐	10	_____
☐	5	_____	☐	11	_____
☐	6	_____	☐	12	_____

B)   Steps / Timeline of Events

☐	1	_____	☐	7	_____
☐	2	_____	☐	8	_____
☐	3	_____	☐	9	_____
☐	4	_____	☐	10	_____
☐	5	_____	☐	11	_____
☐	6	_____	☐	12	_____

C)   People Who Can Help

☐	1	_____	☐	5	_____
☐	2	_____	☐	6	_____
☐	3	_____	☐	7	_____
☐	4	_____	☐	8	_____

D)   Positive BAS

1 _____
2 _____
3 _____
4 _____

E)   Negative BAS

1 _____
2 _____
3 _____
4 _____

F)   Notes / Follow-Up

_____
_____
_____
_____
_____
_____

G)   Next Steps

_____
_____
_____
_____
_____
_____

Goal Sheet

Priority:	Role:

Start Date:	Type of Goal: Daily Short Long	Completion Date:

Goal:	

A)   What do you need to do to obtain this goal? What needs to get done?

1 _____   7 _____
2 _____   8 _____
3 _____   9 _____
4 _____   10 _____
5 _____   11 _____
6 _____   12 _____

B)   Steps / Timeline of Events

1 _____   7 _____
2 _____   8 _____
3 _____   9 _____
4 _____   10 _____
5 _____   11 _____
6 _____   12 _____

C)   People Who Can Help

1 _____   5 _____
2 _____   6 _____
3 _____   7 _____
4 _____   8 _____

D)   Positive BAS

1 _____
2 _____
3 _____
4 _____

E)   Negative BAS

1 _____
2 _____
3 _____
4 _____

F)   Notes / Follow-Up

_____
_____
_____
_____
_____
_____

G)   Next Steps

_____
_____
_____
_____
_____
_____

Goal Sheet

Priority:

Role:

Start Date:

Type of Goal:
Daily   Short   Long

Completion Date:

Goal:

A) **What do you need to do to obtain this goal? What needs to get done?**

1 _____ 7 _____
2 _____ 8 _____
3 _____ 9 _____
4 _____ 10 _____
5 _____ 11 _____
6 _____ 12 _____

B) **Steps / Timeline of Events**

1 _____ 7 _____
2 _____ 8 _____
3 _____ 9 _____
4 _____ 10 _____
5 _____ 11 _____
6 _____ 12 _____

C) **People Who Can Help**

1 _____ 5 _____
2 _____ 6 _____
3 _____ 7 _____
4 _____ 8 _____

D) **Positive BAS**   **E)** **Negative BAS**

1 _____   1 _____
2 _____   2 _____
3 _____   3 _____
4 _____   4 _____

F) **Notes / Follow-Up**   **G)** **Next Steps**

_____   _____
_____   _____
_____   _____
_____   _____
_____   _____
_____   _____

Goal Sheet

Priority:		Role:

Start Date:	Type of Goal: Daily Short Long	Completion Date:

Goal:

A)   What do you need to do to obtain this goal? What needs to get done?

☐ 1 _____	☐ 7 _____
☐ 2 _____	☐ 8 _____
☐ 3 _____	☐ 9 _____
☐ 4 _____	☐ 10 _____
☐ 5 _____	☐ 11 _____
☐ 6 _____	☐ 12 _____

B)   Steps / Timeline of Events

☐ 1 _____	☐ 7 _____
☐ 2 _____	☐ 8 _____
☐ 3 _____	☐ 9 _____
☐ 4 _____	☐ 10 _____
☐ 5 _____	☐ 11 _____
☐ 6 _____	☐ 12 _____

C)   People Who Can Help

☐ 1 _____	☐ 5 _____
☐ 2 _____	☐ 6 _____
☐ 3 _____	☐ 7 _____
☐ 4 _____	☐ 8 _____

D)   Positive BAS

1 _____
2 _____
3 _____
4 _____

E)   Negative BAS

1 _____
2 _____
3 _____
4 _____

F)   Notes / Follow-Up

G)   Next Steps

Goal Sheet

Priority:	Role:

Start Date:	Type of Goal: Daily Short Long	Completion Date:

Goal:

A) <u>What do you need to do to obtain this goal? What needs to get done?</u>

1 _____
2 _____
3 _____
4 _____
5 _____
6 _____

7 _____
8 _____
9 _____
10 _____
11 _____
12 _____

B) <u>Steps / Timeline of Events</u>

1 _____
2 _____
3 _____
4 _____
5 _____
6 _____

7 _____
8 _____
9 _____
10 _____
11 _____
12 _____

C) <u>People Who Can Help</u>

1 _____
2 _____
3 _____
4 _____

5 _____
6 _____
7 _____
8 _____

D) <u>Positive BAS</u>

1 _____
2 _____
3 _____
4 _____

E) <u>Negative BAS</u>

1 _____
2 _____
3 _____
4 _____

F) <u>Notes / Follow-Up</u>

_____
_____
_____
_____
_____
_____

G) <u>Next Steps</u>

_____
_____
_____
_____
_____
_____

Goal Sheet

Priority:	Role:

Start Date:	Type of Goal: Daily Short Long	Completion Date:

Goal:

A)   What do you need to do to obtain this goal? What needs to get done?

☐ 1 _____
☐ 2 _____
☐ 3 _____
☐ 4 _____
☐ 5 _____
☐ 6 _____

☐ 7 _____
☐ 8 _____
☐ 9 _____
☐ 10 _____
☐ 11 _____
☐ 12 _____

B)   Steps / Timeline of Events

☐ 1 _____
☐ 2 _____
☐ 3 _____
☐ 4 _____
☐ 5 _____
☐ 6 _____

☐ 7 _____
☐ 8 _____
☐ 9 _____
☐ 10 _____
☐ 11 _____
☐ 12 _____

C)   People Who Can Help

☐ 1 _____
☐ 2 _____
☐ 3 _____
☐ 4 _____

☐ 5 _____
☐ 6 _____
☐ 7 _____
☐ 8 _____

D)   Positive BAS

1 _____
2 _____
3 _____
4 _____

E)   Negative BAS

1 _____
2 _____
3 _____
4 _____

F)   Notes / Follow-Up

_____
_____
_____
_____
_____
_____

G)   Next Steps

_____
_____
_____
_____
_____
_____

Goal Sheet

Priority:

Role:

Start Date:

Type of Goal:
Daily   Short   Long

Completion Date:

Goal:

A) <u>What do you need to do to obtain this goal? What needs to get done?</u>

1 _____
2 _____
3 _____
4 _____
5 _____
6 _____

7 _____
8 _____
9 _____
10 _____
11 _____
12 _____

B) <u>Steps / Timeline of Events</u>

1 _____
2 _____
3 _____
4 _____
5 _____
6 _____

7 _____
8 _____
9 _____
10 _____
11 _____
12 _____

C) <u>People Who Can Help</u>

1 _____
2 _____
3 _____
4 _____

5 _____
6 _____
7 _____
8 _____

D) <u>Positive BAS</u>

1 _____
2 _____
3 _____
4 _____

E) <u>Negative BAS</u>

1 _____
2 _____
3 _____
4 _____

F) <u>Notes / Follow-Up</u>

_____
_____
_____
_____
_____

G) <u>Next Steps</u>

_____
_____
_____
_____
_____

Goal Sheet

Priority:	Role:

Start Date:	Type of Goal: Daily Short Long	Completion Date:

Goal:

A) What do you need to do to obtain this goal? What needs to get done?

1 _____
2 _____
3 _____
4 _____
5 _____
6 _____

7 _____
8 _____
9 _____
10 _____
11 _____
12 _____

B) Steps / Timeline of Events

1 _____
2 _____
3 _____
4 _____
5 _____
6 _____

7 _____
8 _____
9 _____
10 _____
11 _____
12 _____

C) People Who Can Help

1 _____
2 _____
3 _____
4 _____

5 _____
6 _____
7 _____
8 _____

D) Positive BAS

1 _____
2 _____
3 _____
4 _____

E) Negative BAS

1 _____
2 _____
3 _____
4 _____

F) Notes / Follow-Up

_____
_____
_____
_____
_____
_____

G) Next Steps

_____
_____
_____
_____
_____
_____

Goal Sheet

Priority:

Role:

Start Date:

Type of Goal:
Daily   Short   Long

Completion Date:

Goal:

A) What do you need to do to obtain this goal? What needs to get done?

1 _____
2 _____
3 _____
4 _____
5 _____
6 _____

7 _____
8 _____
9 _____
10 _____
11 _____
12 _____

B) Steps / Timeline of Events

1 _____
2 _____
3 _____
4 _____
5 _____
6 _____

7 _____
8 _____
9 _____
10 _____
11 _____
12 _____

C) People Who Can Help

1 _____
2 _____
3 _____
4 _____

5 _____
6 _____
7 _____
8 _____

D) Positive BAS

1 _____
2 _____
3 _____
4 _____

E) Negative BAS

1 _____
2 _____
3 _____
4 _____

F) Notes / Follow-Up

_____
_____
_____
_____
_____
_____

G) Next Steps

_____
_____
_____
_____
_____
_____